FROM EXCUSES TO EXCURSIONS

HOW I STARTED TRAVELING THE WORLD

THOUGHT
CATALOG
Books

THOUGHT CATALOG BOOKS

Copyright © 2016 by Gloria Atanmo. All rights reserved.

Published by Thought Catalog Books, a division of
The Thought & Expression Co., Williamsburg, Brooklyn.

For general information and submissions:
hello@thoughtcatalog.com

Founded in 2010, Thought Catalog is a website and imprint dedicated to
your ideas and stories. We publish fiction and non-fiction from emerging and
established writers across all genres.

thought.is

Publisher: Chris Lavergne

Art Direction & Design: KJ Parish

Project Manager: Alex Zulauf

ISBN 978-1-945796-19-7

10 9 8 7 6 5 4 3 2 1

FROM EXCUSES to EXCURSIONS

HOW I STARTED TRAVELING * THE WORLD

GLORIA ATANMO

My Mother

To this day, I know you struggle to understand my direction in life. To be honest, I struggle with it, too. You've sacrificed so much for the entire family and you've put all six of us kids in the best position possible to be successful. I wanted nothing more than to make you happy and still do, and although it's not in the way you hoped for, I long for the day when everything will make sense to you. I love you more than words can describe, and I'm blessed to have you in my life.

I was a pain growing up; arguably I still am, yet you continue to support, encourage, and pray for me like the amazing mother you are. Thank you! From halfway across the world, this means so much to me! I can't wait to see you soon. I owe you the world and I'm so happy that you're also slowly getting the chance to see it. I love you.

Lynette Turnbaugh

You became the second mother to me through my most troubled years of life. My high school years were so crucial in the development of who I am today, and to say you played an instrumental part in that is the understatement of the year.

You pushed me when I refused to go further and reached down to help me discover potential I had yet to tap into. It would've been easier to give up on me—to allow me to hang with the wrong people and be influenced by the wrong things. But you never let me get away with mediocrity when it started becoming my best friend.

It's because of you that I take my writing and my love of words so seriously. How I'm able to write so colorfully and descriptively is because of my high-school love affair with figurative language.

Even outside of the classroom, you were a mentor and role model. Your motherly instincts could only be tamed for so long. Thank you for all you've done and continue to do for my growth. You helped me turn my passion for writing into a gateway of opportunities that still opens doors for me today. You mean so much to me and I hope you know I mean every word from the bottom of my heart! XOXO

Baker University

Oh, my dear alma mater. Where do I start? With your professors? With your faculty? Staff? Coaches? Students? Leaders? Stag nights? Haha. In all seriousness, the platform this institution has given me along with the confidence to pursue my passions have done wonders for my career.

I came from Arizona to attend this university, not knowing more than two people. I was given this clean slate to begin adulthood and it came with its challenges, but not nearly as much as its surplus of friends, mentors, and role models.

The family I gained from within this campus and the support system I continue to have from people back in Baldwin City, Kansas just go to show how special of a place this is.

As an alumnus, know that any volunteering, help, or mentorship I can provide to current students is not only a given, but a guarantee and an absolute honor. I'm forever indebted to this place (in more ways than one, haha), and I'm looking forward to the day I can cash in on the hugs and smiles with all the people I've missed over these last few months and years. Thank you all for believing, encouraging, and birthing the global citizen I am today.

TABLE OF CONTENTS

PART ONE

The Dream!

"The Dash"

No matter who you are or where you're from, when it's all said and done, your life will be remembered by three things: the year you were born, the year you died, and the dash in between.

Ever since taking off on this infinite journey abroad, I've set out to create the most adventurous-looking dash I've ever seen.

But my dash started out extremely malformed and bruised. At a young age, society and the media fooled me into believing I was weird. Ironically, I sort of am, but not in the sense that I used to believe.

And because I didn't know how to channel my weirdness, I harbored a lot of negative energy that resulted in petty arguments at school, detentions, suspensions, and near expulsions for most of my teenage years. I know, I know, probably hard for some of you guys to believe if you follow me online now.

I remember when I recently shared the story of my troubled adolescence with a colleague and he warned me that I shouldn't go around telling this to people because they'd judge me. I couldn't understand where he was coming from with that. As if I should paint this false facade of perfection to be respected?

It's actually through my honesty and transparency in my later years that I've been able to develop such deep connections with readers and strangers alike.

And it's because of those humble beginnings and my troubled past that I'm able to appreciate so much of my journey now, because I easily could've been another statistic.

The truth is, we all know where we'd like to be in life (for 99% of us, this is probably somewhere on an exotic beach with Sallie Mae's firstborn washing our feet), but the problem often lies in our confidence in the ability to get there with the vehicle we're currently driving.

Can this job make me enough money to retire by "X" age?

Can this lifestyle grant me the opportunity to live life on my own terms?

Can my sexy husband please do this thing where he starts existing so we can repopulate a nation?

You know, asking the real questions here.

Some people might have more sturdy and financially secure vehicles (aka jobs) that can lead them down the road they hope their 50+ years in the workforce can afford them.

Others might be driving that old-school bucket with a model that ceased production decades ago. Ideally, it's not the most reliable way to get to where you want to go, but a car is a car and you're still getting to your destination faster than the person who would rather sit at home and wait until they have enough money.

In which they eventually buy the vehicle they think will get them to where they want to go. And by then, it's usually too late.

You see, destiny is a crazy concept. I'm supposed to predict my future and take these small steps daily to ensure I get there. Yet if destiny has something else in mind, no matter what I do on my end, fate will eventually play its part...right?

WRONG.

I think fate follows your lead. You can't say you want to do something in life and then never take any steps toward that goal, and then blame it on fate with the lazy excuse that maybe it "just wasn't meant to be" for you to chase that dream.

But OH, WHAT IF IT WAS?

What if you were meant to apply for that position?

What if you were meant to take that trip?

What if you were meant to actually pursue the very thing that keeps you up late at night, dreaming of the day it becomes a reality?

WHAT IF you dared to live a life so terrifying that all your dreams actually came true? WHAT IF?

I ask myself this every day, because I live for this dream and die for this hustle.

I live for the growth. The experiences. The laughs. The pain. The memories. The struggles. The feats. The challenges. The answers. And ultimately, the never-ending questions.

In a world that praises the luck (but not the hustle) and envies the dream (but not the chase), be the outlier.

Have patience in the process and belief in the pursuit because the best part about "living the dream" is knowing how much you sacrificed to get there.

If you live a life so boldly and unapologetically, then life has no choice but to follow suit and command the reciprocation of luck and good karma to work in your favor.

So who am I? Why am I here? And why are you reading this book?

It's simple. I'm nobody special, but I am somebody. Somebody with your interest in mind.

Like many others, the world painted this pretty picture of what my life was supposed to look like if I stayed in school, ate all my vegetables (sorry mom, still not happening), and worked a job to build someone else's dream instead of trying to live my own.

The piece of art was all shiny and labeled with worlds like "financial security" and "The American Dream."

But something about this idea made me itch.

And not like a small tick on your arm, more like a crackhead catching the Holy Ghost. Contradicting, yes, but stay with me here.

Since I was 11 years old, I knew I wanted to be an entrepreneur.

It was career day in Mr. Miranda's class and everyone was asked to go to a table that best described the profession they were most interested in.

Kids dispersed to the tables of doctors, teachers, firemen, lawyers, and more.

Meanwhile, I was left standing in the back, feeling alone, different, and overwhelmed by the number of tables and options, and yet none that accommodated my interests.

What was wrong with me?

After class that day, my teacher pulled me aside as I was fighting back the tears from feeling left out. He told me that despite my attitude and stubbornness, he thought I'd make a great entrepreneur.

I went home that day and researched "entrepreneurship" and at 11 years old, I knew from that day on, that was my destiny and that'd I'd never settle for anything less.

Entrepreneurship became the highlight of my dash, and whether or not you've figured out the highlight of yours, know that it's never too late to begin polishing, coloring, or sharpening the dash of your life that future generations, friends, and family will all remember you by.

Grow your dash.

Know your dash.

OWN YOUR DASH.

"Magic In The Mystery"

L ife is a funny journey, ain't it? We've trained our minds at a young age to believe that failing to plan is planning to fail. We've been told to have this intricately detailed five- and ten-year plan to make sure we never deviate from those paths, but we subsequently freak out when we inevitably do.

Yet and still, I never found a way to think past the outfit I'd be wearing tomorrow.

#MillennialProbs #GirlProbs #ProbsProbs

I've always said my plan is to be SUCCESSFUL. Now, whether or not that's specific enough for you isn't my problem. I think we're pressured at a young age to have this vivid idea of our immediate future to the point that it almost limits and constricts the goals we're capable of achieving.

I want to be successful, but if the route I take to get there changes, I know I'm still on track—some kind of track, at least.

I went through most of my adult years (I'm 26) dibbling and dabbling in all sorts of baskets. Photography, videography, graphic design, web design, blogging, and basketball.

I wouldn't be where I am today if I made a specific plan for myself five years ago and only focused on one of those routes. My accomplishments have been a product of being in the right place and right time with people and opportunities throughout college and beyond.

I got my first taste of traveling abroad in the fall of 2012 as a student at Baker University with a partner school in England called Harlaxton College.

It was there that I first developed my insatiable taste for exploring all things and places foreign and exotic. I was jetting off every weekend with friends and then eventually solo to discover this newfound freedom I was given in a lifestyle that I neither felt I could afford or previously desired.

In college, I always saw those girls who studied abroad and thought, "Oh, good for them." And that they were probably made for that life.

Outside of my regular indulging in French toast and French fries, there was nothing international about me.

The idea of London and Paris sounded cute, but I was more in love with the idea than the reality. College friends who spent semesters abroad told me how much I'd love it and how my personality was made to travel. Those words went in one ear and out the other as I knew I was just too poor to even think about the possibility.

After my first four years at Baker University on a basketball and tennis scholarship and fiddling around with a couple majors, I not only realized I'd need another year to graduate, but that I also would have a first taste of something I'd been longing for—freedom!

My athletic eligibility expires after four years, which meant no 6AM basketball practices, no games, no team obligations, and no one else's schedule I needed to operate on.

Don't get me wrong; I loved being on a team and I miss all of my teammates dearly, but after years of playing, your body and your mind take a toll. I needed a break. I needed a vacation!

Wait—maybe I can study abroad! Maybe I will!

And so it began. I went through the application process, but very nonchalantly, just in case things didn't work out. I didn't want to feel disappointed. Maybe they'll accept me, maybe they won't.

And then I got the letter—accepted! WHOA!

So I took off on August 23rd in 2012 on this unknown and exciting journey that would not only give me my first taste of wanderlust but would eventually turn into the reason I was able to return overseas a year later.

I don't believe in doing things small. And first impressions are something I take very seriously.

I remembered the principal at the time, Gordon Kingsley, coming up to me the second week and saying, "I don't know what it is about you, but you're a force of nature, and I like it." And I made sure to make my presence known and felt since.

I became a Harlaxton Ambassador, a Harlaxton Blogger, and a Harlaxton Resident Assistant within days of arriving. I deliberately put myself in positions to prove my worth as an asset to the institution and subconsciously networked my way into my first job abroad, all while still being a student and traveling most weekends like the others.

A lot of people were quick to throw out the word "lucky"—how "lucky" I was to get this opportunity while failing to realize luck is a byproduct of hard work—or at least its first cousin. But the hard work never gets the praise.

The harder you work, the "luckier" you seem to get, because when there's something you want bad enough, the universe conspires in your favor if your work ethic meets it halfway.

So upon returning back to America from my first four months abroad as a student in 2012, I was so determined to make it back. I worked three jobs and that cute little thing known as a social life just didn't exist. I became a recluse.

Growing up, I've never had a core circle of friends because I never really fit in or could relate to the way the majority thought, acted, or lived.

This scared me for a long time, especially in my adolescent years when fitting in was like reaching gold in life. But I just figured it was me. Something was wrong with me. I found myself developing habits of leaders and having dreams or thoughts that

I could hardly comprehend, let alone verbalize to others to see if they could relate.

I put on a facade for a majority of my life that I was such a social butterfly to disguise the fact that I was so lonely in reality, because I had no one to open up and share my innermost thoughts with.

But when I started traveling, I found myself vulnerably pouring out my heart to complete strangers, knowing I'd probably never see them again, but finding comfort in the purge of my mind until I became confident enough to share them with the world.

And this is why I write. This is why I blog. This is why I no longer seek validation in the form of human approval, but rather write to help others understand that your "weirdness" is what makes you unique, and that's a special gift to the world.

And maybe that's why I'm so addicted to solo travel. The idea of adapting any type of personality I wanted when in a foreign country is so appealing to me—obviously not in a schizophrenic sense, but being able to be me, unapologetically, quirks and all, is an amazing feeling.

I left America for my first job abroad (a media intern at Harlaxton College) at the end of 2013 on a one-way ticket, unsure of when I'd come back, even though the job I had secured was only for six months. I had no idea what the future had in store, but I was willing to do whatever it took to ensure it enabled me to continue living abroad, despite my uncertainties.

But a part of that is liberating. Think about it.

The next chapter of your story is currently being written, and you're holding the pen every morning when you blink your eyes and start a new day. Just like I am.

I feel so excited and blessed to be living this life, even though I couldn't be more uncertain of what's to come next. But man, what an awkwardly awesome feeling that is.

Wherever you are in life, it's okay to not know where to go from there. It's okay to doubt yourself. It's okay to add suspense to this nonfictional best-selling novel that you feel could use an extra chapter or two before your happily ever after.

But while we're so quick to find our happy ending, we forget to enjoy the plot in between and find the magic in the story. Every good storyline needs betrayal, deceit, and heartbreak. Well, I think I can cross off at least two of the three.

There's magic in the mystery, progress in the process, and a reward in the pursuit. Trust your instincts and be your own biggest fan. Your future self will thank you for it.

"Expensive Dreams, Affordable Hustle"

There's nothing wrong with having expensive dreams if you've got an affordable hustle to support that lifestyle.

I've hustled my way from country to country and I was never above picking up random gigs here and there to continue funding my life abroad.

What you all need to realize is that a majority of the digital nomads or people who travel the world full-time are doing some of the most random gigs overseas just to keep traveling.

The notion that we're on an endless vacation is so far from the truth; it's just that whatever job we have, we just might have the Eiffel Tower in the background view. ;)

This list of jobs that I and many other travelers have had abroad includes but isn't limited to:

- — Babysitting/nannying
- — Teaching private English classes
- — Foreign-to-English online translations
- — Travel/social media consulting
- — Freelance writing
- — Working on a cruise ship
- — Au-pairing
- — Becoming a flight attendant
- — Playing a sport overseas

- Working at hostels
- Serving in the Peace Corps
- Becoming a local tour guide
- Bartending
- Modeling
- Travel photography
- Travel blogging

It wasn't until the summer of 2015 where travel blogging actually became a career for me.

Those who knew me before my current hustle might remember my stint with semipro basketball in Barcelona or teaching English and au-pairing around Spain.

What I did was focus on the jobs that were making me money while I grinded away at my travel blog on the side, which didn't bring anything in at the time.

But that didn't matter, because travel blogging was fun for me. It was my escape. It was my baby. It was my way of sharing my reality with the world.

Despite these odd jobs abroad, I can't tell you how frustrating it is to chase after a life with an imagination you know your pockets can't afford.

At the end of the day, all I wanted to do was travel.

Some people have million-dollar dreams with a minimum-wage work ethic, wondering why they can never see past their goals in their head—because that's where they'll stay.

Instead of saving and responsibly spending to fund the life we want, we would rather make these impulsive and unnecessary purchases that later go unused, unwanted, or unnoticed (looking at you, high-waisted denim bell-bottoms from 2005).

Much like our ideas when we don't put them into action, these impulsive purchases become a waste.

I felt a lot of my life revolved around taking risks. That being said, if you're seeking safety or a clean-cut route to fulfill the life you desire, you may want to stop reading here and pass this along to the next daredevil.

I didn't get where I am today by playing it safe or following rules and conforming to the shape others molded for my life. Rather, I created my own three-dimensional lifestyle that was sculpted through trial and error, grit, and a go-getter's mentality.

I want to inspire my fellow daredevils. The ones who choose to live on the edge because anything more than that would be taking up too much space. Those who constantly thrive off the thrill of new adventures and environments. I was that adventure junkie that always needed her fix through a new country or new idea.

But just how do you cope with having dreams you know your pockets can't afford because your bank account is two dollars short from being overdrawn for the second time this month?

How do you wake up every morning fueled by the raw desire for your dreams, yet you never do anything to put them into action?

How do you ensure that your future is secured and that lucrative five-year plan is a notebook flip away?

Simple. You don't.

You need to be willing to do whatever it takes to get where you want to go, despite every factor working against you.

I consider myself a natural-born hustler. I've been hustling since the nurse told my mom my weight out of the womb and I more than likely negotiated it down a couple ounces.

The mentality of a hustler isn't always about money, but it is definitely always about profit and about getting the upper hand, or benefiting from a situation where the reward outweighs the risk.

You can't tell me the name of another first-grader out there who was willing to sell cough drops in kindergarten for chump change. (I was later given time-out in school after being caught. #thuglife)

Even at that young age, I was slangin' nickels and dimes, because that was a valuable amount of money for someone who formerly earned approximately $0.00/week.

We're not going to get into detail about how I had a parent-teacher conference with Mrs. Slauer for this "misdemeanor" because again, I didn't choose the thug life; the thug life chose me.

But instead, we're going to focus on how at seven years old, having my first business shut down didn't stop me from keeping that hustler's mentality.

It was on to my next hustle.

A couple years later, I upgraded to reselling my Lisa Frank collections that I bought from my church with the fake money I'd accumulated for reciting Bible verses, helping put chairs away after service, and winning book-reading contests with my sister—the grind was real, y'all!

So with that faux money, I obtained free goods and valuables from our church's treasure store and was able to resell them at my school and profit off of every single one.

Although I didn't monetarily invest in these colorful, rainbow-diarrhea masterpieces, my hustle allowed me to maximize on them.

In middle school (circa early 2000s), the days of music downloading came to the forefront and I made use of every second of our dial-up connection at the house, oftentimes holding up the phone lines and later being greeted by colorful language in my mother's native Nigerian tongue, Igbo.

This hustle usually required me sitting through entire albums to let it record as I had the Audio Recorder on our Windows desktop open in the background.

I also learned the hard way that I couldn't use the Internet browser during that time either because every sound registered and all my clicks, notifications, and alarms played back in the album of my first unsatisfied and confused customer. Whoops!

Alas, life and business went on. You live and you learn, and I kept improving my services as business grew.

As song requests became more difficult to find and it was hard to keep up with some of the competition I had from my male counterparts, I started to understand the value of marketing—word-of-mouth marketing, to be exact.

I started getting my name out, customizing CD covers, and doing what I could to attract more eyes, and eventually I was doubling my sales and minimizing my work, making multiple CDs for the same mixes and albums. Working smarter, not harder.

Supply equals demand and as long as I had that bootleg dial-up connection back home, I was going to continue making those CDs.

As the Internet and digital world grew with more music software out, business eventually fell by the wayside, but it didn't matter because I was now an adult! Ha, okay, so I was 14—but oh so grown I thought. And this meant I was in high school.

My priorities shifted to basketball and I upgraded/downgraded (depending on your taste) to the exquisite business of Airhead Retail where I literally sold Airhead candy by the twos and threes for 50 cents each. I bought the bulk packs from Costco, which contained 60 Airheads for $9.99. In turn, I made $30 per box and would profit just over 20 bucks per case. Solid numbers.

I guess I should mention that I was easily selling a couple boxes a day to my hungry and bored classmates who found my delicious and colorful treats the perfect distraction from geography and chemistry classes (sorry, teachers).

Some days I had to clump all the Airheads into one large and clear Ziploc bag so that I didn't have to keep running to the trunk of my car when I sold out by second period (a mere two hours into the day).

I have fond memories of passing quarters of change and lip-reading people mouthing the colors they wanted before I passed a couple down the line of the best middlemen classmates a gal could ask for, helping keep business operations smooth.

Life was great. I was bringing in over $200 a week doing absolutely nothing but flashing my goods—Airhead goods, that is—to my peers who knew that lunch was decades away and that chewing on a scrumptious Airhead could, at the time, solve all of life's problems.

When it comes to good business, find a hole and fill it. Do what others aren't doing and provide what others aren't giving.

And then, just like all good hustlers...I was busted. The vice principal approached me with threats of confiscating all my profits and filing a police report because I went against a policy of selling goods on a school campus where only school-sponsored fundraisers were allowed. Oops.

I reasoned that actually, it was funding a school-sponsored activity—my basketball expenses for a tournament we'd be leaving for in a couple months.

Although that was a bald-faced lie, it bought me a warning flag, which my stubborn self took as permission to continue selling until my profits at least totaled $1,000.

And when it happened, I didn't stop.

I got greedy and thought that since I got away with it so far, I could probably rack up at least another $500. That was the dangerous hustler in me.

This probably sounds like chump change to some of you, but understand I never had a job up until that point, so it was beyond me what I could do with that amount of money.

I was trying to maximize this opportunity and figured I could always just ask for forgiveness and forgo permission. So I carried on.

And of course, I got caught...again.

They already had a close eye on me and all it took was one [happy] customer eating their yummy Airhead goods in the open and the colorful Airhead wrapper litter to lead them to believe I was still selling this harmful sugarcoated drug on campus.

So they followed through with the threat and called the cops. True story.

This also might give you an idea of how busy and crime-ridden our town was in Avondale, Arizona.

I was lectured at by a cop who refused to take his sunglasses off indoors (the best kind of people) and after all was said and done, wagged his finger at me and told me this technically wasn't really an offense, but enough of a "crime" to land me a week's worth of detention. (Sorry mom, I never told you about this.)

And because I was actually a straight A student (4.2 GPA), I just used that time to do my homework earlier than usual. So even with my consequences, I didn't take it as a loss, just a lesson.

I share that story to say no matter what your hustle is in life, there will be people who will get in the way of you trying to make things happen. What you're doing won't always be benefiting everyone around you, especially those not contributing to the work, so when they see you profiting, it might upset them.

Don't let the obstacles disguised as people or naysayers lead you to believe that what you're doing is wrong. If you're not harming yourself or anybody else with your hustle (outside of premature diabetes, I suppose), then don't let other people rain on your sugarcoated parade.

I don't remember what I used all that money to buy, and I'm sure it wasn't something smart, given my overnight rise to riches (ha), but I'll never forget the empowerment I felt from having my own stream of revenue not handed to me by someone else who tried to control how I worked or operated. I was my own boss. I dealt with my customers directly. I controlled my income.

It was something as basic as selling candy, yet as profitable as the average part-time job a teenager at that age would receive by probably working twice as many hours in environments that were half as welcoming.

That hustler's mentality stayed with me throughout my college years where I started and successfully anchored my first legitimate business in photography and graphic design.

The audacity and boldness to take that leap forward, diving in headfirst, and coming up for air later, was the beginning of a series of decisions I'd make involving risks and going against the odds.

Again, it doesn't matter how expensive your dreams are when you've got an affordable hustle to get you there. Even if that hustle is colorful and delicious.

"Your Debt Is Not Your Destiny"

The biggest thing stopping most people from turning travel from a goal into a reality is money.

But why do we give so much power to money? Sure, it's a means to an end, but money won't fully fund your dreams. It's audacity that will.

Along with debt, obstacles will come. And they will suck. But that doesn't mean you need to abandon ship! You change your route, not your destination. Delay doesn't mean denial, and a triumph is twice as rewarding with a trial en route.

When I booked a one-way ticket to Barcelona after my UK visa expired back in the summer of 2014, I was pretty much up against a wall.

I had just $100 to my name, but I didn't let that stop me from cutting my dreams short.

The average and perhaps rational person would wait until they found a job and then go to a foreign country under the right circumstances. I'm irrational, impulsive, and incredibly dangerous when it comes to pursuing my dreams, and I simply refused to let my excuses or my lack of funds get in the way.

Again, your debt is NOT your destiny. And if you're waiting for the right circumstances to travel, the flying pigs will be out and dancing to the melodies of the fat ladies singing before you know it.

Some things you have to just do and figure out later. I've had many nights of confusion, tears, and frustration in Spain, because life happens to everyone no matter what and I chose to rise to the occasion each time, and I'm a better person because of it.

I went to Barcelona with basically pennies to my name and a blog I was ready to give up on.

My precious blog's domain was set to expire just a day after I arrived in Barcelona. I got there on $15 and needed to pay $75 for the blog renewal.

Again, the person who sees the Almighty Dollar as the ulterior motive would have quit on that blog.

But I was way too resourceful to allow having $15 in my pockets hinder my hustle.

Between au-pairing, English teaching, online translations, freelance writing, and a semipro basketball gig, I was back on my feet in no time.

Two years later and my blog is now my full-time job. I've been featured in popular online publications such as Huffington Post, Matador Network, Thought Catalog, Elite Daily, Essence, BuzzFeed, and more.

And I can't tell you it all started when I took the leap of moving to Spain. But I can tell you that it started by taking a leap SOME-WHERE.

You might not know where you're going. You might question every step of the way. But the important thing is to move. Somewhere. Somehow. In the direction of your dreams. Whether you know what you're doing or not.

If you become a slave to a dollar amount, you will never truly be free.

"Death To The 5-Year Plan"

So what exactly is my 5-year plan? Well...I guess I'll let you know when I have one! My 5-year plan, or lack thereof rather, is something that's being hammered into the minds of young adults to make sure their future is adequately planned for. At least that's what I assume, because I've never really taken it seriously. Lol, oops.

I don't even know where I'll be next month, let alone five years from now! I am, however, all about planning, setting goals, and ensuring that you have options ahead of you so you're not stuck on a path to nowhere.

So I'm not going to tell you why you shouldn't have a 5-year plan, because there is a good purpose behind it, and I encourage college graduates especially to make one.

I'm instead going tell you why I don't have one and why I will never put that kind of pressure on myself.

So much of my life has been a ball of opportunity and randomness ricocheting in a room of faith, luck, and risks. I've never once claimed to have life figured out. I'm as unstable as they get, honestly. I'll have an idea of what I want to do with my life one minute, and it'll completely change by the next. With the 72-tab browser my mind operates on, it's a bit chaotic up there.

While being 26 is relatively young in the grand scheme of things, I've found that the greatest opportunities and biggest adventures come to those who mix a little bit of fear with faith in the unknown.

If you told me five years ago that I'd be living and working abroad, amassing a passport of 40 countries across four continents, I'd ask for a sip of what you were drinking, because it must be strong!

I'm constantly meeting new people and seeking new opportunities to the point where a 5-year plan would only feel constricting to me. Once you cross the pond and get the slightest taste of how big and amazing this world is, it'd be silly to want to settle for anything less than a life full of adventure.

Life is too short and my imagination is too big to limit myself to a one-track-minded lifestyle. I've become so addicted to the thrill of meeting new people in unfamiliar territory, discovering historical ties, and making cultural exchanges with people who I've never seen outside of international news broadcast networks.

So if you asked me where I'll be in five years, you'll find out exactly when I do—five years from now. I know that I want to be successful and happy, but I'm not going to limit the ways and avenues whereby I can get there.

I've worked my whole life to put myself in a position to be successful, so why would I let the corporate world marginalize that? I've always had an entrepreneurial spirit and I think it's both exciting and terrifying to live life embracing whatever comes your way.

I want to get from A to B, but if I have to algebraically incorporate letters and different formulas to get my solution, I'm okay with that! It's okay to let 1+1 equal 11, especially when you suck at math to begin with, ha.

They say you gotta network to get work, and I have a bit of shamelessness when it comes to professing my ignorance in an area in order to attain the knowledge needed to propel me to the next level. There's nothing wrong with not having all the answers. Honestly, I hope to never have all the answers. Maintaining a student mentality and constantly being on a journey to learn more is what will keep life exciting for me.

If you're in college, a recent graduate, or heck, even twice my age, there is still time to make something more of your life. I can't speak for everyone who's traveled abroad, but if you put yourself out into the world, it'll spark and light a fire in you that you never thought was flammable.

Every time I get an opportunity to travel to unknown territory, I promise you I'm the kid in the candy store, toy factory, and amusement park all at once.

So if your 5-year plan stresses you out as it is, try not having one at all. The liberation, anxiety, and thrill are enough to fuel the energy you'll need to be guided in the right direction. Trust your intuition and always be open to new opportunities. The worst that can come from it all is a lesson. And even then, one can argue experience is the best way to learn!

From my 0-year plan to yours, here's to the calculated risk-takers. May you never stop challenging yourself for more.

"My American Dream: Outside Of America"

It's funny, because as an American, you keep hearing about this cliché "American Dream" that's supposed to define the ultimate sign of making it big in this country.

Get you a nice ol' job. Get you a nice li'l degree. Get you a white-picket fence. Then take the first job you're offered out of college. Use that money to buy a nice car. Rushingly get married. Anxiously reproduce. Become a slave to the dollar. Live above your means to impress people you don't care about. Repeat that step enough times to rack up considerable debt. Cry. Die. The end.

I know, I know—irresistible, right?!

So you can imagine my need to flee from the rat race known as the "American Dream," which sounded more like the American Nightmare.

Don't get me wrong; I love my country. I love America and everything we stand for—bacon and freedom. Not necessarily in that order, but ya know.

It's just a bit ironic that I'm living my American Dream outside of America.

Millennials today are no longer settling for material things that fade and standard jobs that lack the fulfillment they crave.

The average American is okay with the first option. And why shouldn't they be? It's safe, it's convenient, and it's deemed socially responsible.

But I'm not here to knock people who love their desk job any more than I am to encourage those who hate theirs.

Be okay accepting the fact that a majority of you guys reading this were destined for greater things in life. You were destined to be, do, see, and feel more.

The day I stopped letting this scare me and allowed it to fuel me, my life went from a ball of confusion to a party of opportunities.

So what is my dream?

Ultimately, to live where and how I please. To dictate my days and spend my time doing things that fulfill my purpose in this world. To understand other cultures. To inspire others to travel. To bring out the best in people who can only see their worst. To be all that God created me to be and more. That is my American Dream.

"Adventure Is Dangerous, But Routine Is Lethal"

The number of times blog readers and friends would send me messages and emails out of concern for my safety when I announced I was crossing into country x, y, or z was more than I could keep track of.

To them, the further east I went, the more in danger I put myself, thanks to sensationalized media that filled in when our firsthand experiences couldn't.

So by some people's standards, yes, I live a dangerous life.

But you know what was more dangerous and deadly to me than that?

Routine.

Never wanting to challenge or push myself beyond the comfortable palette of colors I was given to paint with.

There's nothing more detrimental to our success than ourselves. We get in the way of our own potential and growth by being complacent and settling for things that don't make us happy.

I escaped the routine 9-5 life not because I didn't like work.

Heck, I arguably work twice as much as the average person in America to be able to sustain this lifestyle.

But since I was a teenager, I knew I would be the most unemployable employee ever.

I was (and still am) stubborn, impulsive, and a ball of risks waiting to explode.

You see, I'd work a 9 to 9 if it meant I could live my life on my own terms.

The idea of someone else dictating when I should start work, have lunch, and ultimately be valued monetarily is something I'm not willing to subject myself to.

As a woman especially, stating my value used to terrify me. But the minute I started using my worth as a sword to lead with, rather than a shield to hide behind, I knew it was history from there.

I know I'd be the hardest worker in the building, but I'd make a terrible employee. I'd much rather grind 24 hours a day toward my own goals than work even one hour slaving away toward someone else's.

I think it takes a special type of person to sit in a cubicle and take orders from a higher authority with complete contentment.

Don't get me wrong; entrepreneurship isn't for everyone. And we need people in this world who can do the day-to-day tasks. If everyone is a leader and no one follows, nothing gets done.

So if you're a follower, thanks for tuning in, but know this next bit isn't directed at you.

I want to talk to my leaders and my rebels for a second. The ones who are tired of trying to fit in when they were born to stand out.

You've never quite had a problem getting a job because companies would love to have you. But you're a ball of risks in every sense of the word. And here's why employers might be better off choosing otherwise:

---

1 — *They need someone who will follow their rules without diverging too far left or right.*

Rules are made to be broken (especially when it comes to serving suggestions on Nutella jars).

In all seriousness, some of the world's greatest leaders were known as rebels early in their careers. They knew how suppressed and unfulfilled their lives would be if they were only able to do things exactly the way they were told.

This isn't to say I won't get the job done; I absolutely will. But I'll probably add another component to it, just like the last time.

And you will probably love it.

---

2 — *They need someone who will behave appropriately.*

Everything about me is inappropriate.

From my sense of humor to the layer of accessories I need to complete my ensemble.

I will laugh too loud. I will smile too hard. I will be way too emotionally invested in our projects, and you don't need that kind of clinginess in the workforce.

---

3 — *They need someone who tolerates working in groups.*

Group projects have proven time and time again to be nothing short of a slow and painful death. I'd love for every group member I've worked with to be the ones carrying my coffin at my funeral so they can let me down one last time.

Somewhere along the way of the created definition of "group work" was a genius who insisted that this must entail one person who never shows up, one person who is slightly incompetent, one person who has "the best ideas in the world," and the last poor soul who picks up the slack for the prior three.

I refuse to put myself through this inexplicable pain yet again.

> *4 — They need someone they can give a set of tasks to and trust they'll be done by the end of the day.*

I can do this; I really can.

But this comes with the need to surf websites for inspiration and take coffee breaks—perhaps even the occasional dance break.

This is my routine for kicking the midday slump. And I can only stay seated for so long.

God bless chairs. They are arguably one of the greatest inventions ever. They allow our feet to take a momentary break while we play hide-and-go-seek with our brain cells while binge-watching reality TV.

They're works of art, and yet I must part ways with them regularly. Sorry, chair. It's not me, it's you.

> *5 — They need someone who can follow directions without asking questions.*

Not only will I question your intentions, but I will have the consumer in mind. If they're being shorthanded in any way, how is that something I can remain silent about?

The big companies can get away with murder, and as someone who has worked on both sides of the fence, I can't simply sit on top of it and watch the madness on either side.

> *6 — They need someone who likes their ideas the most.*

I have too many ideas, and I might want to try them all. In fact, I will.

I must, I need to, just to make sure I don't let a genius thought get away.

We spend hours trapped inside our head, alone with our thoughts. That could either be extremely terrifying or really inspiring.

If you're a creative person, you always have a notepad handy to jot down your scribbles when those fleeting moments of inspiration come to you at the most random hours of the day.

You know you can envision and successfully execute an idea when given the adequate amount of time and the inspiration and motivation are maintained.

But if your boss has an idea, you're forced to like it and run with it, while yours becomes an afterthought.

---

7 — They need someone to work for them.

I would rather work with you, not for you.

Isn't it so fulfilling watching your life and dreams slip away from you while you pour all your energy out investing in someone else's vision? You're making them rich off your labor while you're profiting a minuscule percentage of the millions they make at the top.

The fact is that despite my work ethic, I'll be paid an amount that gives me just enough to afford to continue living and keeping up with the rat race.

---

8 — They need someone who's okay with their hourly wage.

I am one of the few people who'd rather take commission over hourly pay. You will never see the true colors of someone's work ethic until you put him or her in a situation where he or she can only earn from the work that actually gets done.

The average worker might be able to efficiently wash three cars in one hour. The hard worker can double that and efficiently wash six in the same time frame. Yet the latter is getting the same hourly pay as the former.

This should infuriate the hustler.

---

9 — They need someone who's normal.

I've never been normal a day in my life, and I couldn't be more happy about that.

Sure, I conform to certain societal norms, but on the inside, there's a rebel crafting world domination by way of peculiar habits, overly ambitious goals, and a surplus of wine.

There's a new version of the American Dream which consists of getting to see the world and travel while you work.

I can't sit still. I must breathe the air of new cities, flirt with the customs of new cultures, and dance so far outside my comfort zone that anything inside of it feels foreign.

---

10 — They need someone who will always be on time.

There's a reason "deadlines" have the word "dead" in them. You're hardly capable of producing a pulse after rushing to get that company analysis or financial report in.

There's an adrenaline that comes with finishing your job, time and time again, moments before it's due.

Will it always be your best work? Debatable.

But remember, you're already an overachiever, so your average work is just in line with the best work of others. Oh, the advantages of being a hustler!

Since I was 11 years old, I knew I wanted to be an entrepreneur. And after truly understanding what it was during career day, I knew it was my destiny. And I've fought for it since.

Entrepreneurship is and can be whatever you want it to be. In a world where people love to tell you everything you can't do in life, show them instead everything you can do.

Adventure is dangerous, but routine is lethal. So I'll continue taking my chances.

"Excuses: Rescuing Those Who Don't Want It Bad Enough"

We all make excuses. Some, arguably better than others. Growing up, I was the queen of this. I knew what to say and how to say it, to justify reasons why life didn't quite work out.

Why I didn't get that position.

Why I wasn't on time.

Why I couldn't sink those two clutch free throws in what could've been our one and only win against our rival Tolleson High back when I played at La Joya.

So many failures. Yet time and time again, I got really good at justifying them.

But in reality, excuses are lazy and unfair to those who actually believe in your potential. You're capable of doing everything you set your mind to. But why do people have to tell us this before we actually believe it?

The worst part about excuses is that they affect more than just you. They affect your time and the time of those who believe in you, too.

Time is free to have but expensive to waste!

It's the one thing we all lose but can never get back.

There's a saying that goes, "You hate on my grind like you don't have the same 24 hours" and that ain't nothin' but the truth served with a side of large fries, honey!

How funny, unfair, and ironic would it be if some people had 24 hours in a day, while others had 12, and another group had only six?

How crucial would your time be if you fell into the latter category, running out of hours daily to accomplish the things you wanted to do?

How much time would you then have for those dear excuses you make on a daily basis?

There are people that operate with the mindset of the six-hour crowd while they live on a planet where the 24-hour-a-day rule applies to everyone.

I can empathize with mothers, people who work two or three jobs, and so on. There are just circumstances and situations that put others at a handicap more than other groups.

But the word "excuses" is in the title because I'm here to help you find ways to turn them around and manifest them into excursions, results, and success.

The minute you start falling victim to your circumstances is the minute you let the world dictate how high you can climb on this mountain of life.

Sure, some people started their climb years before you and some might have better shoes and equipment for stability, but we're all climbing different mountains here. The important thing is not to get distracted by what others are doing, what they are wearing, and how they're using their tools to reach their mountaintop.

You're on a different climb. A different path. With a different set of circumstances. Your comparisons do no justice!

I'll use traveling as an example. The biggest excuse I hear about why people can't travel is that they can't afford to. And then I'd get snide remarks from friends who were clearly more well-off financially than I was, wondering how [a peasant like me] could afford it when they couldn't.

I wrote an article that later went viral on Huffington Post, Matador Network, and Elite Daily and basically there was no gray area. People either loved it or they hated it (and me, haha), but it resonated well with many people because they were able to relate.

It basically came down to prioritization. And here's the article below:

Whenever someone asks me how I afford to travel, I have to force myself not to respond with "selling Nutella by the spoonful and procrastinating Sallie Mae payments."

It's just so funny because people think there's this magic formula out there. This one-size-fits-all encompassing route that gives everyone an equal chance of seeing the world.

But our equal chances don't mean we have an equal will or stubbornness to pursue traveling further than just a wish.

What if I told you a small puppy died every time you asked someone how they afforded to travel?

How would you feel about the graveyard of dog souls you've single-handedly dug out of curiosity for someone else's wallet?

For shame, I say. For shame.

Ask anybody who travels, or travel bloggers in particular, how they feel about this question and I guarantee a large majority of them will say the same as I'm about to.

And let me preface by stating that I absolutely love getting emails from you guys with specific questions, which I always answer to the best of my ability, so please don't take this personally!

Best friends and strangers have asked this question and I hold it against no one, but here's the thing you guys might not realize when you ask someone how they can afford to travel. I've broken it down in three points.

Problem #1

It insinuates that traveling is expensive to begin with.

I've said this before and I'll say it again. TRAVELING IS ONLY EXPENSIVE WHEN IT'S AS CONVENIENT AS POSSIBLE. You're paying for convenience when you book a flight on a specific day, nonstop, first-class, and with a beverage included. All that sounds great, but if a commercial ticket on the cheapest flying date of the week (Tuesday) could manage its way on your schedule, choose that instead!

But I do understand when the average working American has a two-week space in a year that they could use for travel, it limits the flexibility.

I'm also very transparent about the fact that living and working abroad for an extended amount of time is by far the best and cheapest way to travel more and further.

With Europe for example, if you're already based on this continent, you have budget airlines, cross-country rail systems, international buses, and so much more that all give you multiple options and very affordable ways to travel. Like how it only cost me $100 for a round-trip journey from Barcelona through the French Riviera with stops in Montpellier, Marseille, Saint-Tropez, Nice, and Monaco. I kid you not. Less than $100 for all transportation costs.

Problem #2

It suggests that you're too lazy to do your own research.

A simple Google search of "How can you afford to travel?" will yield golden results like budgeting tips, how to start a travel fund, and cheapest destinations around the world.

Approximately 87.3 million results from this search. And somehow I turn into a search box and get questions such as "What countries are nearby Spain?" to my inbox. Lol, does my Google work faster than yours? I don't get it.

I love you guys to death. I really do. But when you're able to do basic and fundamental research first, and then come to me with more specific questions to yield specific results, everybody's happy.

I didn't get where I am today by emailing every entrepreneur asking them broad and general things like "How can I make as much money as you?" or "How can I be as successful as you?" Those are vague questions and everybody's circumstances in life are so different that my path won't be identical to theirs or yours.

I get that you want a personal anecdote from someone you know or follow, but snooping around beforehand does volumes. The person on the receiving end is not only more likely to respond more quickly, but they can also target your response in a way that most benefits you and your current situation.

From garnering a general idea of opportunities and paths people take that allow them to travel, it could lead to more substantial questions like, "Do you recommend a specific teaching program?" or "What's the biggest expense you cut back on?" or even "What was the first step you took to begin traveling?" These questions are so much easier, simpler, and honestly, more fun to answer!

Inversely, I may downplay how easy and affordable it is to travel, because I haven't booked a flight for more than $100 in such a long time. And I still have to remind myself that not everybody knows that I could fly to Switzerland for $30 next week from Barcelona if I wanted.

Not everyone is aware of European budget airlines. And not everyone takes into consideration that if you take the size of the U.S. and put it next to Europe, country-hopping in Europe is no different than state-hopping in North America. It's all about perspective.

EasyJet.com has this amazing feature where you can set your budget, and it'll show you all the places you can fly for under that price. So for under $40, I could fly to over 15 cities in France, Italy, Germany, Switzerland, and the United Kingdom. That is CHUMP change. That's dinner for two at a restaurant. That's a full week of Starbucks. That's almost a full tank of gas on a regular basis. PERSPECTIVE, GUYS!

Problem #3

It belittles the idea that you can actually manage your funds, start a savings account, and allocate money accordingly.

Think about the things you love and things you decide to allocate a good chunk of your money to. When I say a good chunk, I'm going to take an average flight out of Barcelona during peak tourist season, so anywhere between $35 and $75.

Imagine if I flipped the script and started asking people about the things they were passionate about or spent money on in the manner that they asked me.

"Wow, Britney! How can you afford to get your nails done every week? I wish I could do that, too!"

"Yo, Duncan! How do you afford season tickets for the Kansas City Chiefs? Livin' the dream, bruh!"

"Hey, Julia! So tell me again how you can afford that Michael Kors watch? Please teach me your ways! You must be soooooooo lucky! I wish I had your life!"

"OMG, Parker! How can you afford to eat out at restaurants every day? How long did it take you to save up for this?"

"Hey, Kaci! Just wondering how you could afford all of your Starbucks coffees every day? Do your parents help pay for all of this?"

These are standard costs that you spend on a regular basis, yet nobody questions it. It's just a way you've chosen to spend your money. So why is spending money on travel any different?

There is no magic. There is no formula. Just research, will, and determination.

The point of this is to help you guys understand that there are so many ways and resources to fund your travels if you really want to. I get that our generation is all about the instant-gratification life and we want to just send a two-minute email to a travel blogger in hopes for a response on how to start jet-setting by next week, but I'm afraid it's not that simple.

There are several resources, tips, and hacks on how I've funded travels spread throughout my blog if you use the "find" tool on the home page, browse other sites, and do a little bit of research the same way I did to help create a path that worked for my specific circumstances! And then feel free to ask questions from there! I want to help you guys, I really do! But you gotta meet me halfway. I'll put the gas in your car, but eventually you gotta put the pedal to the metal and start driving on your own. :)

Over 100,000 shares and republished in five languages across multiple platforms later, and my world exploded.

If you're new to the language of sarcasm, I can see how this might've come off as harsh or offensive, but I honestly meant it from a good place.

If I didn't like helping others, I wouldn't dedicate my entire life, blog, and resources like these showing people ways to make it more affordable for them!

The hate comments I also received made me lose approximately 2.5 minutes of sleep at night. People were maaaaad. Like BIG mad. Reasonably so. People are defensive when it comes to confrontation and shutting down their excuses. It's a daily battle for some and an hourly one for others, but at the end of the day, you are your own biggest obstacle.

You can let the excuses you make ru(i)n your life, or you can start taking action, hold yourself accountable, and accomplish your goals, and not without obstacles, but despite them!

"Running Away From Sallie Mae"

First off, if you don't know who Sallie Mae is, then you, my friend, are living the true American Dream.

Non-Americans might be wondering who exactly Sallie Mae is and why 90% of college graduates have her at the top of their hit lists.

I'm not going to get into the statistics of what the average American's student loan debt is from going to university or how many generations after their kids are born will be stuck paying it, but I will say that it's definitely a problem.

It's a problem for so many of us and I hate the fact that it stifles people from living a life pursuing their dreams.

The truth is, I'm really just on a mission to outrun Sallie Mae and hope that I die before she catches up to me. Some wishful thinking there, but this is a judgment-free zone. I hope.

In all honesty, it's entirely possible to continue living your life while being a responsible adult. I wouldn't know, because I fail at the adulting part, but I've seen it on the Internet, so it must be true!

The fact of the matter is, if you let your student debt rule your life and block your dreams, then it will do exactly that. And many allow it and think they're being responsible.

And while I commend those who refuse to travel until all their debt is paid off, I just want to remind you guys that where there's a will, there's still a way to do both.

You can make little sacrifices at home that allow you to give up small comforts and luxuries to be able to continue paying your bills, but not at the expense of the life you want to live.

For me, that was finding a way to continue traveling.

Goodbye, Netflix.

Goodbye, Spotify.

Goodbye, social life. I can't afford your highway robbery in the disguise of cocktails and club entrances anymore.

Tell your money where to go instead of wondering where it went.

The secret to having it all is believing you already do. It's not by comparing your journey with someone else's or making someone else's funds or priorities any of your business.

Again, it's not money that funds your dreams. It's audacity. Courage. Tenacity. The intangibles of downright hard work and a nonstop grind. Sure, money will help build your dreams, but it sure as hell won't support them on their own.

There are millionaires who go bankrupt because they lack the qualities of a determined soul who values the pursuit more than the prize.

I think there's this illusion that only rich people can build the life they dream of.

Newsflash, guys: I am NOT rich. In fact, I don't claim to have any more money than you. I probably don't. You can blame my impulsive jet-setting tendencies for this as well as my expensively unhealthy Nutella addiction.

What I do have, though, is a goal in mind. And a work ethic that would knock out Tyson if matched up in the ring.

That's right, Mike Tython. Leth thee what you goth.

When it comes to doing what you love, you shouldn't think there is anybody else working harder than you at your craft. And it's not even about a comparison to someone else, either. It's about knowing that the average person stays motivated for about as long as a *Game of Thrones* episode. If you want to achieve your goals, it needs to be a relentless and daily pursuit.

So I don't know what it is your heart desires, but if you let another day go by without chasing after what you want in life, then maybe you don't want it as badly as you think.

Priorities are EVERYTHING. If you didn't eat out for a whole month and saved that money instead, what if I told you that's enough to book a vacation somewhere? Enough to buy the domain and hosting for a website you've wanted to make for your business? Enough to attend that professional training workshop to take your skills to the next level?

So what is it you want to do? Where is it you want to go? And when will you turn that wish into a reality by taking the necessary steps to get there? Time will pass, anyway; might as well spend the one life you have doing what makes you happy.

It's never the end of the world when there's evidence that you've at least tried to reach your goals, regardless if you did or not. My failures don't define me any more than my successes do. But hey...what do I know, anyway? (Everything, of course.)

So while I've got a round and brown cheek that I'd like Sallie Mae to smooch, I'll continue outrunning her in the meantime.

"Travel Is The New Black"

What I love about this industry is that it's here to stay. Travel isn't trendy, because it will always be popular. As long as this planet, different countries, and modes of transportation exist, so will travel. And so will our need to discover and fulfill our wanderlust through it.

I remember a time when Paris could only be associated with things such as the Eiffel Tower (or Isaac Tower if you're my mother—this makes for a great story in person, just remind me), loaves of bread, and barrels of wine.

All equally amazing, but having been to Paris on five separate occasions during five different phases of my life, I'm now able to remember it by more than just its cliché monuments.

I remember it by the comedy show I went to see that poked fun at its confusing system they try to label as the Metro.

I remember it by the charming Frenchman who took me on a bike ride through the city just as the night started to fall and for the first time ever, I thought I was in a movie, being whisked away by this gorgeous man, treated to dinner and a late-night stroll by the River Seine, only to remember the next day how these indescribable and short-lived encounters are one of the many downsides to this lifestyle.

I remember it by the time I accidentally walked into the Tour de France, yes THE Tour de France, as a large crowd gathered by the Arc de Triomphe to chant, cheer, and catch glimpses of these daring athletes who were braving the last leg of the race.

And I'll especially remember it by the cutest encounter I had with a Ukrainian lady.

I was going about my day, strolling through the crowd to take a breather, because Eiffel Tower selfies are exhausting and I'm out of shape.

So I pop onto a ledge nearby only to have a security officer come wag his finger and say, "C'est impossible!" which is hilarious and typical of French authority. Their answer for everything is usually, "It's impossible" when they really just mean "No."

Anyways, I hop down and say, "Désolé!" ("Sorry!") with a slight grunt in my tone to pass off as a local. I think he thought I was sick.

So it forces me to pass by the couple again. I kept seeing the woman glance at me and just smile. Of course I smile back and moments later her husband asks me shyly, "Uhhm, are you a blogger?"

Now at the time, this had only ever happened twice before—someone recognizing my face from "The Internet"—scary, lol. So I nod hesitantly, remembering my first Xanga account and hoping they're not somehow referring to those glory days.

So he told his wife and she squeals with excitement, signaling with a couple jumps up and down that she knows my blog and then asks for a photo.

Her husband said she didn't speak much English, so our conversation exchanges were a series of smiles, hugs, and laughter (my first language, anyway). I learned that they're traveling wedding photographers that just shot a wedding in a small village south of Paris and were on their way back home that evening.

We went for coffee afterward and exchanged life stories in the usual manner when I meet new people for the first time. The connection was so authentic and it was absolutely the highlight of my day. And that is what Paris means to me now.

Travel is not only the best thing you can do for yourself in terms of growth, perspective, and eternal gain, but it's something that you can spend money on and never feel like there's a loss.

It's the gift that keeps on giving and lives on through memories, pictures, and stories.

For the people who don't think travel is for them, let me just tell you this.

I once was you, too. I never desired or felt the need to see anything outside of what I already knew.

But traveling in your country compared to outside of it is like the experience of swimming in a pool vs. an ocean. Sure, they're both water and you're getting your feet wet regardless, but can you really say that the experience is the same?

I didn't think so.

PART TWO

The Journey!

"Things To Consider Before Moving Abroad"

More and more people are starting to pick up on the secret of how to afford and fund long-term travel. The fact of the matter is, if you want to travel longer and further than ever before, you simply need to spend a period of time living and working abroad.

A continent like Europe, where countries are connected through several modes of transportation, means that a two-hour flight north, east, south, or west would probably land you in another country.

With the euro (€) at a decade low and the US dollar ($) at a decade high, you're getting more bang for your buck on travel expenses such as accommodation, flights, and food. So now that you're about 90% convinced that a year abroad is exactly what you need to refresh your perspective and find your zest for life again, somehow the idea of the big move is still just a tad bit overwhelming.

So we're about to do some soul-searching to determine if this is indeed exactly what you want for your life. Be honest with yourself, because it's you that you're trying to convince after all... not anyone else.

If you're considering moving abroad, whether temporarily, permanently, or "however-arily," there are definitive ways to help ease the transition.

Of course, I can only speak from my own experience, and there are so many "If I knew then what I know now" moments, but I think these are all key things to consider before you make the big move!

Learn A New Language

One thing you'll come to appreciate about Europeans especially is their ability to speak more than one language, and fluently. And then occasionally, you'll meet the modern-day Superman who can speak about five or six. It's truly remarkable.

Learning another language will help open doors of opportunities you can land while abroad and of course lead to great conversations with locals. With Spanish for example, if I'd given it a serious attempt in high school and maybe watched five more episodes of *Dora the Explorer,* who knows how much more fluent I'd be? I'll tell you—lots. Going to the city and immersing yourself in the culture is arguably one of the best ways to learn the language, but you will do yourself a favor if you can be halfway fluent upon arrival!

Get Your Phone Unlocked

I was skeptical about this at first, because I didn't want to "go against the book" and mess with the phone's system. But I came to find out there's actually nothing wrong with this process and most cell phone companies in America have a service to do this for you.

You'll save SO much money if you see yourself being abroad for at least a year. I got my phone unlocked in England for about $20 (a one-time fee), and was able to get a British SIM card put in my phone so that I could still use my Samsung Galaxy that I bought in America as a local phone with a local number.

And when I lived in Spain, I was also able to get a new Spanish SIM card for a whopping $10 and BOOM, I'm good to go again, because my phone was unlocked and could accept any SIM around the world.

Without an unlocked phone, you're looking at triple-digit costs in obtaining a number to work with your phone or having to buy a new phone and contract altogether.

Change Your Spending Habits

There are certain things called "comfort items" that we spend money on in the States. These "luxuries" add up and fade just as quickly as a $50 meal exits your bowels in a couple hours. Instead of always splurging on those expensive shoes and that Michael Kors watch that you absolutely must have to show your financial status on social media, consider for a moment that buying experiences rather than "stuff" will be far more valuable in the future.

At the end of the day, our graves will all look the same and nothing goes with you when you're six feet under. Invest in the bare essentials and things that truly matter and you'll realize that saving for that trip to London that sounded like a one-year ordeal will only take a few months when you make the right changes in your spending.

Invest More Time In Doing What You Love

This one is something I preach day in and day out. What good is your time if you're not spending it doing something fulfilling or something that makes you happy? I understand bills need to be paid, but little by little, give yourself the time you deserve to learn more about what you love and how to fine-tune that craft.

If I never spent the 75% of my freshman year having late-night rendezvous in the library to have sexy dates with the 21-inch iMac computers with all the applications a graphic/web designer could dream of, I would have never taught myself how to build websites or how to do graphic design. Small, humble steps of research, Google, and YouTube tutorials five years ago, and now I never have to worry about ever contracting a person to build a website or design something for me because I can do all that by myself.

Also, my photography is a self-taught hustle through trial and error that has more than doubled the salary of any regular job I've ever had back in America. You'd be surprised how much these skill sets turn into side hustles while you're abroad. In this day and age, we'd be foolish not to take advantage of our technologically advanced generation who grew up in a digital age, which has virtually made us walking assets to companies that need the tech-savvy skills we possess.

Start A Blog Or Journal
(For Non-Monetary Purposes)

This is for the person who sees themselves being abroad for at least three months or more. I think having a blog is the best way to chronicle the amazing experience you'll have as well as share and exchange your journey with the several other wanderers you'll meet on your travels.

Having a blog also opens doors for local businesses and organizations to partner with you and offer discounts or free perks in exchange for promotion. But if you don't see yourself wanting to publicize your journey as much, at least buy a diary where you can privately document your thoughts and track your growth. You will thank yourself later.

Don't Come Looking For Love

This alone can be a book by itself, ha. The age-old saying goes that things will come to you the minute you stop looking for them. It's no secret most girls who've gone abroad have coveted the fantasy of finding their Prince Charming with an accent they comprehend 10% of, elope on some exotic island, and then produce the hottest babies known to man. This "happily-ever-after" is actually a "sadly-never-again" because 99.99999% of the time, it will never work out like that.

Being abroad doesn't mean you need to be A BROAD. (Can we take a moment to see what I did there?) However, there's absolutely nothing wrong with entertaining potential, but the minute you start chasing it, longing for it, and depending on it, you turn into that girl.

Don't be that girl.

If you met a guy at the same bar all the study-abroad students frequent every weekend, then honey, you know this ain't his first rodeo. Are you falling for the man or falling for the fantasy? Are you meeting his parents or meeting his mattress? Go abroad and let this journey be about finding YOU, not a significant other. You're welcome in advance.

Start The Visa Process Very Early. Like, Yesterday!

How do I put this in a way to not scare you? Hmmm...basically the visa process is equivalent to booking a one-way ticket to hell. There will be tears. Lots of them.

You will find yourself broke halfway through because they find ways to drain you dry of every dollar and coin you've ever made. They then pierce those wounds with confusion that reaches the very fiber of your soul, testing every ounce of sanity you thought you owned.

The good thing is, with lots of time, several reads through the fine print, a couple glasses of wine, the blood of a firstborn, and prayer, you will survive, and when you do, you'll have stories for days for your kids' kids.

After taking all these things into consideration, now it's time to ask yourself the real questions to help turn this into a reality.

How independent do you consider yourself?

Does the thought of being on your own scare you or excite you? Do you always need someone to help get you out of sticky situations? Can you go more than a year without being in a relationship?

These are serious things you need to consider, because no one will hold your hand through job searches, visa paperwork, or breakups. Life happens to everyone, whether in the comfort of your hometown or halfway across the world. I've had to cry on my own shoulder, pick up broken pieces, and figure out plans many times on my own. It's all a part of your journey and you become so much stronger in the end. But know that this part of the journey is inevitable, so be ready when it comes.

What do you want to gain from this experience?

Besides seeing as many places as is humanly possible, traveling without a purpose will leave you emptier than your wallet. You want to make sure you're doing this for the right reasons. Not to find love. Not to make your friends jealous. And not to make your liver hate you forever (although that's a byproduct of this lifestyle). You need to find the deeper value in what you're about to embark on so that you don't come back with your money depleted and an opportunity wasted.

---

1 — How will you fund yourself/travels?

In between traveling, you need to find a side hustle. What can you do or offer others to help sustain yourself on your travels? Do you own a digital camera? Are you a social media guru? Do you have a musical talent? Can you sing? Can you paint? Are you multilingual? All these are legitimate skills that can earn you side money whether on the streets or doing freelance gigs for a major business or company. Never rely on just one income when living abroad, because you'll need a backup for your backup when your backup is backed up, ha.

---

2 — *What's your Plan B? No, not that kind. I HOPE.*

If you're like me, your Plan B might be to keep trying Plan A until it works. This is by the book, the actual definition of insanity, and I'm 100% okay with that. But again, life has a funny way of working out sometimes, and you need to be prepared to switch gears and take a detour if that's necessary.

---

3 — *What is one thing you've always wanted to do before you die?*

And can this be fulfilled while traveling? What better time to do this while on the road creating memories of a lifetime anyway? I think there's a liberation you gain from traveling in general, and that idea that we should wait for the right time to reach our goals is something that people take to their grave and never end up fulfilling. Use this time abroad to accomplish as many of your bucket list items as possible!

---

4 — *How can this experience impact your next chapter?*

How can you use this experience to land your next job or plan your next trip? How can you format this on your resumé or CV to make this experience look like a million bucks to a potential employer? Never underestimate the power of life abroad when talking to CEOs upon your return. That experience says so much more on paper than a 4.0 GPA, and there's a global market for just about anything these days. Network to get work, my friend.

---

5 — Will the job you have now still be there when you return?

If the answer is yes, then good. If the answer is no, then even better! Chances are, you're in a job you're not too passionate about anyway. It pays the bills and gets you by, but do you rush to get out of bed every morning?

Didn't think so.

---

6 — What "luxuries" can you cut back on now to help pay for the flight and initial cash to get you on your feet after the move?

You'd be surprised how little you actually need to survive. It's crazy, but there was actually a time Starbucks didn't exist. Or nail salons. Or overpriced gym memberships. But someway, somehow, people managed.

Cut back on your Starbucks coffee and brew your own at home. Quit the nail pampering and buy $5 polish that will last you over two months. Cancel the gym membership that you haven't used in a year and buy a home workout DVD and a couple weights and bring the gym to you. BOOM! What's up, new savings of $300/ month? I see you!

And most importantly—are you ready for your life to be changed forever? To take the good with the bad and remember that no matter what happens, this experience, this moment, and this journey is something you wouldn't trade for the world (oh hey, irony!)?

It's hard to imagine what I thought of the world and life in general before my almost 40 countries of globetrotting so effortlessly ripped my mind apart. It tore up all the narrow-minded stereotypes and replaced them with gems of light, compassion, and understanding, to help me see people and life with a new perspective. Life abroad is every bit what you make of it. And I choose to make this life nothing short of extraordinary.

"Is It Worth It?"

Is it worth it?

The answer is YES.
The lost sleep.
The failures.
The sacrifices.
The doubt.
The risks.
The criticism.
The judgments.
The struggles.
The detours.
The dangers.
The decisions.

All to live the life some people can only dream of. I'd do it all over again even if you doubled the hardships, because in the end, there will be the days of glory. In your very own self-made paradise, you can look back on your journey and be proud of the path you created.

Yes, there will be tough times. But there will also be you. Standing victorious. In the end. Every. Single. Time.

"The Empowerment Of Solo Travel"

Ahh, yes. The question that always rears its head into every conversation with every new person I meet. It's no secret that I'm a small-talk enthusiast, and when you're breaking the ice and learning general information about a person, as well as asking questions that led to the current reasoning behind their existence in front of you at that very moment in time, the question, "Wait... so you travel all by yourself?" always finds its way to center stage.

"Wait, like ALL alone?" "Like, ALL by yourself?"

If you can imagine their tone in those questions, please imagine me mimicking it in my answer. It's 2016 and it's amazing what society still deems as taboo for women.

But the biggest concern about all of this is, am I safe? How exactly can I ensure my safety? Are my testicle-kicking skills up to par? Yes, yes, and you better believe, YES. And I will address all of those later, because the reality is you can never be 100% safe anywhere.

Whether surrounded by all your loved ones or in the middle of nowhere in a foreign country, danger has no biases. And whether in your hometown or halfway across the world, you're at risk daily anyway. So the mentality of fearing for your safety really needs to be a mental shift and acceptance that you can only control so much.

As a solo traveler, it's such a liberating feeling to wander the streets of a foreign country by yourself knowing that you can get into as much or as little madness as you feel like!

So why is it that I feel so confident and safe on my solo journeys? It's simple. I'm not stupid. I don't put myself in situations or surround myself with people who give off even the slightest bit of a suspicious vibe. I'm a strong believer in being responsible for the energy you bring and keep around you.

When traveling alone, your faith in humanity is constantly restored by the Good Samaritans, generous souls, and kindhearted people from around the world who are always willing to help you with directions or simply offer the best thing a person halfway across the world can—an enlightening and intellectual conversation.

So my advice to any aspiring solo traveler out there is to use your own good conscience to be safe and never put yourself in a situation where it can potentially be compromised.

Adventure is out there, waiting for you to grab its hand and lead it somewhere new! Just remember that being fun and being stupid do NOT have to be synonymous.

"The Unequivocal Education Of Travel"

When I checked off Country #15 back in June of 2014, I was reminded how traveling is really the best form of education. It's raw. It's real. But most importantly, it challenges the information we've been spoon-fed all our lives. To learn is to live. And traveling is living in its purest form.

But what it does to you is synonymous to the effects of school. Sometimes you're given a test, whether you're ready for it or not. It'll be thrown at you like a bag of bricks, giving some people a black eye from the experience and others a backbone.

I've learned that knowledge is as powerful as the intent in which you choose to use it. Feed your brain to broaden your perspective. I've never met someone who's traveled and came back more closed-minded.

What you're doing, in essence, is expanding the space in your head with new experiences. And the best way to understand a culture is to dine with them, laugh with them, and learn from them. And lately, I've been fortunate enough to do all three.

Travel is simply the best education out there.

"Couchsurfing 101"

When it comes to finding ways to save money on the road, there hasn't been a more useful resource than Couchsurfing.com.

If you're unfamiliar with the concept, it's basically a network of travelers, hosts, guests, and everyone in between who provide a community of good karma for those who wish to partake in it responsibly.

There are hosts around the world who open up their homes to travelers, and travelers around the world who get hosted by locals. It's a two-way street in terms of trust, and the website is as regulated as possible with prior guests and hosts able to leave references and feedback on people's profile for others to check.

After surfing in well over fifteen countries around Europe, I've easily saved upwards of $2-3K of what should've been spent on living, transportation, and food expenses because of the lovely, generous, and hospitable people that fill this network.

I first joined while I was studying abroad in England in 2012, out of pure skepticism, desperation, and curiosity.

A few of my gal pals told me about it and I of course resorted to cynicism, because I had only been abroad for a couple weeks up until that point. Everything I knew about Europe was from what I saw or learned from the media—aka the worst possible source ever.

It wasn't until I gave it a shot in Liverpool that I knew I'd just discovered gold in travel currency. I'd just found a way to explore a new city, save money, and make new friends. Basically, I was sold!

What Couchsurfing provides that a normal hostel or hotel doesn't is a stay with a local who is as vulnerable as you are. To welcome a complete stranger into your home and to stay in a stranger's home honestly isn't something I'd ever do in America.

But why was I so willing all of a sudden to try this overseas?

There's a certain hospitality the European continent is known for, and it's not something I can explain adequately until you experience it for yourself.

Being fed, transported, and provided for, all in exchange for some answers about my culture and company around town, is incredible.

I know some of you are still iffy about this concept, and it's definitely not for everyone.

Sleep on strangers' couches and be the inspiration behind *Taken 8* (or whatever number sequel they're forcing in theaters these days).

It's crazy how we've become a product of our consumption of violence and homicide from movies and video games.

Even with the word "stranger," our minds are programmed to think of these people as STRANGE or weird.

Here's the honest-to-God truth that any American who's studied or lived abroad for an extended amount of time will tell you.

We feel safer in foreign countries than we do in America.

The bottom line is that the European culture I've been met with has a "strangely" hospitable way of living. People cooking you the food from their fridge, giving you the clothes off their back (well, closet) just because they want you to have a souvenir, people taking off work, or even better, inviting their colleagues to come meet you over dinner and drinks.

The fact of the matter is people abroad (just like us) sometimes fall victim to the mass media brainwashing and stereotypes. They've never met an American in person before, so their fascination with our culture, our music, and our strange obsession with the wrong kind of "football" is incredible to them.

They love exchanging stories and getting firsthand travel advice about what to see in America, because visiting the states is a dream for 95% of the foreigners you'll meet.

And any time I can tell them that America is more than Vegas, New York, and LA, then I feel like I've done my job as a U.S. citizen, haha. But seriously, #BoycottVegas.

Plain and simple, Couchsurfing, although a free service, is really about a cultural exchange when it comes to currency. A local opens up their home to you in hopes that you can open up your heart to them.

Let them learn about your country, your life, your identity, and your story that brought you to the very moment you're sharing—whether or not that moment be taking a tipsy stroll down a mazed road, stumbling upon a cathedral, and feeling the sudden urge to practice your nonexistent ballet skills (true story: Montpellier, France).

These kinds of authentic and random memories are what turn a tourist into a traveler.

And when you think about a majority of tourists, they're only interested in seeing the top attractions that Google neatly compiled with an array of "top 10" article must-sees on the first page of a Google search. Imagine the hundreds of thousands of people who typed in the same thing, got the same results, and had the same mundane, neatly packaged experience as you did.

People don't realize all the gems they're missing out on because the bigwig companies were able to buy their way to the top of Google searches and leave all the others by the wayside.

But think about it—who knows a country or city better than someone who's lived there all their life? Fall back, Google. I'm gonna take their word on this one.

Not only do you have free accommodation, but you have a free tour guide at your service as well. And because of them, I've been led to hidden beaches, tasted local-grown foods, and danced the night away at urban clubs where I bypassed the line and walked right into thanks to my host being a regular there.

Some of your hosts even have cars and offer to play taxi for the day and spend time taking you to all their favorite spots or any highlights you want to see.

And sometimes you get to meet even more travelers if your host has more space for others.

And don't let the word "couch" fool you, because more times than not, I've actually had a room and bathroom to myself and more privacy than a hostel would've given, and all at no cost.

And just like BlaBlaCar, AirBnB, and other community services, past guests leave reviews of their stay there.

My advice, especially to women, is don't be stupid. However, this is a general rule that I encourage everyone to apply to anything in life, really, ha.

But when it comes to female solo travelers, try to stay with other women, couples, or hosts who are also hosting other people.

Use your common sense when looking at profiles and reviews, and never be the guinea pig. If someone doesn't have a review yet because they're new, I wouldn't take those chances.

As guests, it's also important to remember these people are doing YOU a favor by opening up their homes to a "stranger." Some might even meet you at a nearby train station with the spare keys and tell you to enjoy your stay and take off somewhere for the weekend (true story, London 2014, the trust in the community is amazing).

But in general, the people on Couchsurfing are extremely hospitable souls. It's a community of good karma, because they build a network of friends and travelers all over the world who will reciprocate the hospitality if they ever visited their respective hometowns.

I've been very lucky to have stayed in nicer and more expensive flats most of the time, but I understand that won't always be the case. So don't be the high-maintenance brat who nitpicks or complains about everything. Remember, they don't owe you anything!

And since it is free, a token of appreciation by bringing a bottle of wine or something from your home country is a nice way to get things off to a good start. In terms of sending requests to potential hosts, use your good judgment.

I understand you're short on time and it feels ever-so-convenient to copy and paste the same message to about twenty people, but it's incredibly tacky, especially when you address all of them to "Stefan," showing you clearly took no time to go through and personalize any of them.

It takes five minutes to skim a person's profile, check out their interests, see what you guys have in common, check for any red flags in the references, and get a general vibe from them.

When sending a request, always address them by their name and introduce yourself! A quick two-to-three-sentence intro about who you are and why you'll be in their city is a good start.

You can then bring up similarities and ask about some of their favorite things to do, suggesting that even if they can't host, you will still have a bit of a local's perspective.

It definitely helps to throw in the fact that you understand how many requests they get a day and that even meeting up for coffee would suffice, showing that you're not desperate for a free place to crash but would genuinely like to meet with a local.

What a lot of hosts do is put keywords or phrases in their profile asking to share your favorite city or type of food in your request so that they know you actually read their profile. All a host has to do is check for the key words in your message and if it's not there, the request gets ignored.

I did an experiment while living in Barcelona and changed my profile to where I was accepting guests.

I was receiving around 50-60 new requests a day. It was awful, lol. Very obvious copy and paste messages with no proof of even glancing twice at the information on my page.

I also had English as my preferred language, but because I lived in Barcelona, people assumed I only spoke Spanish (without checking my profile) and started apologizing for their poor levels of Spanish or using Google Translate and sending a message in Spanish when they could've seen that English is my native language.

I took it a step further and put in the first line of my profile something along the lines of how I will throw them off a mountain, or something equally terrifying and ridiculous. And that they needed to tell me what mountain I should throw them off of in their message request.

Not one single person told me which mountain they wanted to end their life over. It was horrific. How can people be so careless?! I NEEDED TO KNOW WHICH MOUNTAINS THEY WOULD FALL TO THEIR DEATHS FROM!

Never be so desperate to save a few bucks that you compromise your safety.

As this network is 90% filled with awesome people, don't accidentally let one of the 10% slip through by not doing your due diligence first and reading the profiles of the hosts you are messaging!

"A Passport Of Purpose"

Strive to impact, not impress. Traveling is truly an amazing concept. Not many other things in life can leave you speechless, yet turn you into a storyteller. But traveling does just that and more, depending on your attitude and aptitude to let it make an imprint greater than just the stamp in your passport.

From my first year's worth of travel, I went from a passport of pages to a passport of purpose, as the stamps through my first 15 countries of exploration decorated the empty spaces, silently singing the stories of spontaneous adventures, life-changing encounters, and the everlasting impact the people from other cultures had on me.

But the biggest thing I had to learn was how to be a traveler and not a tourist. The minute you master this, the floodgates of opportunity and discovery will open for you, because there's a special component to traveling with purpose that changes the way you see and approach life.

Try to create unique experiences by going outside the norm to visit places under the radar. Break out of your shell by trying to speak the language and exchanging perspectives and cultural views with locals.

As a global citizen, your duty is to enrich this world. People need you. We need you. I need you—to continue to push the agenda for the uniquely born, free-spirited adventure junkies who eat bowls of pride and courage for breakfast every morning. With a side of bacon. Cuz, 'Murica!

When it comes to doing what you love or achieving your goals, it needs to be a relentless and daily pursuit. A friend asked me the other day, "Glo, what keeps you going?" I didn't think "coffee" sufficed as an answer, so I explained how I never let the good get to my head or the bad get to my heart. If you stay true to yourself and always find the good in the worst of situations, every day becomes a blessing. Change your thinking. Change your life.

Again, my failures don't define me any more than my successes do.

What does define me are the homeless people I've interacted with in Spain, the backpackers I met that surprised me with a home-cooked dinner one night in France, the lady I chatted with while climbing a mountain who later invited me over for tea in Scotland, dancing down the middle of the street and inviting people to join me in Belgium, watching a sunset from 1,000 feet in the air in Hungary, pretending to like rugby while trying to make sense of said sport in Ireland, awkwardly avoiding eye contact with hot guys on the Metro in Germany, trespassing through private property to get a perfect picture in Greece, posing for pictures with babies while walking through Romania, giving hugs to strangers in London, and overall, just returning from a trip more enlightened, enriched, and fulfilled than I was before.

So what will you travel with? A passport of pages or a passport of purpose?

"Being Black Abroad: A Minority Of A Minority"

The first time it happened, I didn't jump to share it on social media.

I mean, it was pretty embarrassing. I was mortified. I had my dignity stripped away from me, and there was nothing I could do about it.

I'm talking about the time I was mistaken for a prostitute while traveling. And not just once.

But let me tell you about the first time it happened—in Prague.

And maybe this is partially my fault, as one of the Cardinal Rules of traveling is to try not to set your expectations of a place too high based on other people's experiences. That way you're always pleasantly surprised. But the stream of comments about how Prague was everyone's "favorite city" flooded my notifications, and resist I could not. The anticipation was real.

Now first off, Prague is BEAUTIFUL. It's warm, charming, and absolutely breathtaking in the squares. Some streets don't even look real because they're so picturesque. This is what I expected, and my aesthetic needs were graciously met.

But here's where things took a turn.

I did my usual wandering in my usual aimless manner. When traveling in general, I make an effort to blend in when I can, but I usually adhere to my typical bohemian attire—blouse, scarf, fedora, and bracelets.

Nothing about what I was wearing or how I looked should've drawn the attention that I got. The attention I'm referring to is something every black American abroad has experienced in some manner before.

The lack of multiculturalism caused me to be a walking exhibit straight out of a museum.

Here are the four variations of stares you get as a black American abroad.

1 — *The Look Of Curiosity*

This face is quite harmless, because there's a very good chance that they may have never seen a black person up close and in person before. So you being their first encounter has sparked all kinds of questions and innermost thoughts translating into their current gaze of wonder. They might genuinely ask if you're related to the Obamas, and once they mentally convince themselves otherwise, you kindly tell them you're only second cousins with the president and that it's been a couple of years since you've last been able to meet at a family reunion.

2 — *The Look Of Approval*

This face is the most inviting of them all. They clearly look at you and take a few seconds to glance over your black features (wide nose, big lips, hair texture) and come to the acknowledgement that you're exactly how they imagined "your kind" to be. They give you a big smile, they ask you slightly intruding questions, and they overall show their pleasure to welcome you to their city. For the record, there was not a single look of approval I received in Prague, but I've definitely received them in different parts of Poland, France, Greece, Ireland, Scotland, Italy, Croatia, Montenegro, Cyprus, and Jordan.

---

3 — *The Look Of Disgust*

This face hurts. Not so much the action of them making the face, but more so the lack of concern to try to hide or disguise their expression in the first place. It's like they're saying they're not okay with my presence, but instead of keeping that pleasant thought to themselves, they want to make sure I'm aware of it, too. These stares were plentiful in Prague. It was disheartening because I had such high hopes.

In all honesty, this almost always comes from the older generations. People who were kids when the Wright Brothers made it possible to sit in a chair in the sky and teleport yourself to foreign territory. So the concept of multiculturalism and leisure travel is something their generation was never engulfed in like this one.

---

4 — *The Look Of Objectification/Sexualization*

This face is one I know female travelers experience everywhere and I'm not comparing our struggle in this department, but I know that black women specifically get objectifying stares in certain regions much more than anyone else. This is due to the increasing amount of African migrant women who turn to prostitution when it's the only work they can find outside of their native country. The local culture then accepts this as the norm and they associate anyone resembling a woman of African descent to follow suit.

And before anyone tries to tell me to "appreciate the stares while they're still coming," let me kindly tell you "NO." Here's why.

There's this thing called mutual respect, and as long as you don't give me a reason to treat you like the chauvinistic masochist that you come off as, then you will get the kind and chipper Glo.

Staring is not a compliment. It's rude. Whether it's a look of fascination or disgust, the act is so uncomfortable for the person on the receiving end, and even while making it very apparent that I, too, have these things called eyes that allow me to stare back, they continue in their glare.

The worst part of all of this was walking on the sidewalk and having car after car slow down, honk, or the strangest, put a hand up and point toward the end of the street, either signaling to meet them at the corner, or God knows what else. I felt so out of my element. I couldn't be my normal, happy-go-lucky self.

To top my day off, I was at a stoplight with a girl who would be considered gorgeous by today's societal standards: brunette, long hair, toned legs, and wearing a mini dress.

Now, I don't go around sticking prostitute labels on pretty people like some locals do when they see foreigners, but between the two of us, if one of us were more dressed for the job, 1, 2, 3— NOT IT!

Regardless, guess who got the harassment as a car with two men in the front pulled up to the crosswalk? She was invisible. They looked right at me, muttered some words, smirked, and I felt them practically undressing me with their eyes. It was disgusting and I felt so violated.

I'm fully aware there will be creeps, jerks, and losers in every city or country regardless of where you are. But to feel like I got a taste of each collectively while in Prague didn't sit well with me.

I'm not defeated enough to never visit again; I just know that I will do my best whenever I travel to use every experience, both good and bad, to humble myself. They don't see my degree. They don't see my self-made business. They don't see the world of knowledge I have to offer on the surface.

Leaving town, the last person that stared at me (in disgust), I made sure I smiled back. Because whatever preconceived notions Western media and news had convinced them into thinking I'm not deserving of any reciprocation of the smiles and kindness I give first, then I'll make sure that if I'm the only black person they ever encounter, that their experience is a pleasant one.

And maybe if they stopped gaping at me like I escaped from a museum and used their words to engage in the cultural exchanges I've grown to love about traveling, we could slowly chip away at the stereotypes we hold of cultures we've never met in person. This is why I travel. And this is why you should, too.

Fast-forward a year later where I'm now a full-time travel blogger and this is my daily conversation.

"Can you tell me what place is safe to travel for a black person?" I read in an all too familiar email I get from yet another African-American, which is now the fastest growing demographic of U.S. travelers.

"SAFE" AND "BLACK."

I typed those two words into my inbox and it rendered eight pages of emails.

Perhaps the second most popular question I answer on a regular basis.

The fact that black people have to ensure their safety because of the inherent threat people on a global scale automatically assume is why my voice (and other minority voices) are so important in the travelsphere.

When it comes to privilege, white privilege in particular, people can be so defensive about it.

But listen to this closely: WHITE PRIVILEGE IS NOT SOMETHING TO FEEL GUILTY ABOUT.

I repeat: WHITE PRIVILEGE SHOULD NOT MAKE YOU FEEL GUILTY.

It's when you don't acknowledge white privilege exists that it becomes a problem.

White privilege, for example, is the ability to travel to any European country without fear that your race or religion will get you misjudged or discriminated against on a micro or macro level.

I was chatting with a lovely Greek woman in her mid-30s the other day, and she told me that growing up, there was one single black family in her neighborhood.

She never saw them, but she heard of them. LOL, Greek mythology anyone? ;)

So later on in life, in her 20s, when she saw one up close for the first time, she said, and I quote, "I couldn't believe it! It was like magic! I was just so shocked that they were real and right in front of me!"

Now you might laugh or shake your head, but Americans who for the most part have the opportunity to grow up in diverse neighborhoods don't realize that's not the reality for so many cities and countries abroad.

So of course, I cracked up, because I've been on the receiving end of people seeing a black person for the first time MANY times during my travels, and this type of reaction is pretty amusing.

So when white people try to use the argument, "But I don't see color, we're all one!" it's dismissive and counterproductive.

OF COURSE YOU SEE COLOR. Heck, I WANT you to see my color. I'm black and I'm proud, got damnit!

It's when you use my color against me to be prejudiced where I draw the line.

If a green-skinned race of people started to emerge, you know good and well we would all notice.

We're not color blind. Our minds just don't work like that—they're programmed to see color.

It's getting people to reprogram their mind to see color yet NOT react in fear, negativity, or hate, that the world and closed-minded people need to work on.

One of the proudest things about having a travel blog as a minority is that I'm able to shed some light on places with my firsthand perspectives for the black community and others with darker skin tones.

The blogging world is saturated with white bloggers, like many other industries, which is why it's so important for minorities to be represented across the board so that they can continue serving as a voice to a community of people that can't relate to the language of certain privileges that others speak in.

And while the way you're treated abroad is indeed a combination of how you present yourself, how much of an effort you make to acclimate to the local culture, and maybe even the time of the year you're there, a large part will also be based on where people think you're from before you open your mouth.

The first impression before the first impression.

They see your color and their brain starts shifting into media mode, collecting all the data they've seen from movies and the news, and then you open your mouth and a warm and educated tone comes out, and you can see some struggling to process that.

The reality of black travel is that there will always be a region of the world where you go and are immediately perceived as dangerous or promiscuous.

Dangerous, in regards to the black male thug representation—thanks, media!

Promiscuous, due to the hyper-sexualization of the black female body in the past and even in today's society.

The fetishizing of black skin color is why I turn down dates.

It's why I can't wait at bus stops at night because cars will pull over, asking for my rates. Rome, Barcelona, Prague, yep. Still very common in those cities.

On that same note, there are many places that treat African-Americans better than they treat Africans, and that's something I need to be more vocal about, too. Because that's not okay, either.

When something has never affected you or will never be a part of your daily conversation/experience, it's easy to dismiss the issue as exaggerated or fabricated.

But I hope these conversations become easier and easier to have as racism ain't leaving this planet anytime soon.

So the more comfortable we are dissecting the truths around its existence and dispelling stereotypes of entire diasporas, the sooner we can unite in our differences to see our similarities.

The human race is one, but the unfortunate reality is, that statement is a privilege not everyone gets to experience.

"The Price Of Living The Dream"

While I'm 100% aware of how fortunate and blessed I feel every morning to wake up and do what never really feels like work, I think there's a voice missing from the conversation that's so important, especially if you've ever found yourself scrolling through my or another traveler's Instagram feed feeling inadequate about your own life.

Whether to my face or to my inbox, I hear that I'm "living the dream" every single day, and while I try to be excited about confirming their observation, I can't help but cringe inside, because I don't think people really take into account how much of a price is paid to live said "dream."

Like anything worth having in life, there will be trials, obstacles, and roadblocks, but most importantly, fears that usually hinder most from the initial pursuit.

And while I know several others "living the dream" might not feel as comfortable talking about the negative aspects of this lifestyle, y'all know I'm an open book (sometimes literally, t'hehe), and I always try to foster inspiration from my transparency more than anything else.

Living the dream ultimately comes at a price, but I knew it was one I was willing to pay. But what exactly are those costs and sacrifices? Let me try to break it down in cute terms.

For any writer starting out, the first time you press "publish" on a piece of your innermost thoughts, you're opening yourself up to a world of criticism, and the thought makes you want to sh*t yourself, which I don't recommend, however tempting/gratifying it may sound.

And this is where Stay-At-Home-Steve and Hate-The-World-Holly come out of the woodworks to nitpick and criticize every waking detail about your articles, your travels, or even your outfits. Like, seriously? What did my $5 thrift-store top do to draw such negativity from Nancy-The-Nobody?

Strangers feel entitled to tell you how much you suck, and this is hoping they even read past the title of your articles, because newsflash: Most won't.

They'll channel their inner jealousy into half-coherent thoughts, and they'll stalk every single social media channel you have to remind you how much they can't stand you. It's so adorable.

While some may call that borderline obsessed, I just hope it's not too late for somebody to hug them in life. They're just deprived and I'm confident their happiness is a few bear hugs away. Keep searching for those standing cuddles, my laughable lilies. Somebody in this world loves you. It ain't me. But hey, somebody!

The most recent hate mail I got was actually pretty funny. A gal found my Instagram and proceeded to flood my inbox with several questions, haphazardly, lacking any sort of fluidity.

When I suggested she send me one big email with all her messages so I can answer accordingly, she scoffed and literally sent me eight separate emails, each a copy and paste of the individual messages she originally sent, defeating the purpose of sending an email to begin with.

WHY DO PEOPLE LIKE YOU EXIST?

But alas, I had some downtime (read: alcohol), so I got back to her a day later with some general tips, pointers, and linked her to articles where I wrote answers to the very questions she had, in detail and everything.

Her response?

"I didn't write you so that you could link me to articles. I wrote you so that you could answer me directly."

She is so lucky I found Jesus. She never heard from me again and I blocked her on Instagram to make sure she didn't benefit from any more free information I posted.

#ByeFelicia
#YouAreDismissed
#HaveSeveralSeats
#TakeTheWheelFatherGod
#ForgiveHerSinsJesus

The Payment Of Pressure

There's this inherent pressure from being a travel blogger or content creator that makes you feel like you should always be doing something.

You need to always be engaging with your audience. You need to always be pumping out content. You need to always be "on," and I simply can't be that person.

I'll burn myself out and I'm okay with not flying my Wonder Woman cape for a few days to fall into a sleep coma and pretend adulthood is more of an aspiration than a reality.

Not to mention, I'm a ball of estrogen, throwing myself into a world that continues to manhandle me in the best way possible (hey-ohhh!), loving me and leaving me, as I find myself falling head over heels with cities that I have to break up with a few days later.

And if you think traveling solves your problems, lol, that's cute.

If anything, it exposes them. Because if you have anger problems at home, try having those same issues in a country where you don't speak the local language.

But it's okay to allow yourself to have your human moments, take a break from social media, or go on an emotional rant about something that tugs strongly at your heart.

But no matter what you do or what you say, people will always be watching, and you have to make sure to exercise caution and responsibility with the platform you've built.

It's actually the people that aren't showing up in your notifications that are watching you the most—and that's what makes things tricky. Lurkers be lurkin', yo.

And while I don't want to be held to a higher standard than the next 26-year-old, I understand it comes with the territory, and that's something I try to work on daily.

But sometimes, it's just easier to say F&% IT. As in, FIX IT. Jesus. What were you thinking?

The Funds Of Freedom

If you've never had to chase a company down for six months because they "forgot" to pay you, man, you really oughta live life more on the edge! Ha.

Don't get me started on the companies that pay you on a 90-day cycle. "Thanks for all the work you did for us in February! Here's your check!" *deposits in June*

In a saturated industry of newbies throwing free work to brands left and right in hopes for sponsored work down the line, you have to constantly justify your worth when you get daily emails from marketers trying to access your audience "without a budget." Oh, the joys!

As you've spent years fostering an engaged community, perfecting your Instagram gallery, or just mastering your writing, photography, or digital ninja skills, that's a tangible thing that you put your creativity into and 100% deserves adequate compensation for.

But Marketing-Maven-Marsha still thinks that exposure to her [unengaged] 500 Facebook fans is a fair trade. Oy.

Mix tedious back-and-forth negotiating with chasing down months-old payments, and it makes for a hell of a stress-free life, am I right?

I've learned the hard way that I needed to start requiring half the payment upfront, and while you will probably sound like a pain for that (and sometimes they will let you know it, ha), it's a small step in the right direction of asserting yourself as a business[wo]man.

But when you first start out navigating the waters of entrepreneurship and digital nomadness, the amount of times you have to reach inside your magic hat to pull out a random number that defines something you've dedicated the better part of your life to will happen more times than you can count.

And sure, we might be able to wake up when we want, but we're also never really not working...if that makes sense.

You see, if you have a 9-5, you can essentially disregard any and all work-related things when your foot is not inside that office.

But because digital nomads have no office, everywhere is essentially our workplace. And while I'd like to pretend I'm one of those people who spends hours on the beach, laptop handy, goodness gracious, have you guys tried playing damage control when sand gets on your laptop?

Have you ever felt your laptop overheating from being in the sun so long and subsequently burning your thighs to feel like the grilled meat you never knew they were?

How do people even see the screen when the sun is glaring right over it? Questions That Need Answers For 500, Alex.

I don't think I've ever been productive working at the beach, but hey, lemme post this sessy-ass photo to the 'gram 'gram anyway, because hashtag, LIFE GOALS for the peasants!

But it's really not about that. And that's why I try to shed light on it when I can.

Speaking of downsides, anybody wanna take a peek at my savings account? Like, what is that even? Yo no hablo the language of savings.

But if the nightmare sacrifices are still worth the dream life, then I absolutely encourage you to pursue it! Again, I wouldn't trade this life for anything, and the day this all starts feeling like work is the day I'll have to sit down and reconsider the direction of my life. But alas, the wheels have not fallen off, so this bad boy will keep on truckin'.

So yes, I may be "living the dream," but I hope you can also see that beyond the beauty of this journey there will be chaos, struggles, and failures, but ironically enough, I'm able to see the beauty in that, too. ;)

"48 Hours Of Starvation"

I'd be lying if I said I didn't think this day would come. I knew it would. I just didn't think it'd happen so soon. A mere seven days after I announced I'd be taking my travel blogging on the road full-time and be completely nomadic.

How embarrassing.

It wasn't a matter of not having money, but more so a miscommunication, a non-budgeted last-minute expense, and voodoo dolls with my face on them drowning in water to begin what turned into the worst experience I ever had abroad.

I was arriving in Berlin from Amsterdam high on life (no, not that kind), but everything I had heard about Berlin from friends was about how much I'd love it and how they could totally see me living there.

But my excitement would soon turn to panic as I found myself at the train station, tortured by the beeping sound of my card declining as I was trying to buy a measly $3 ticket from the bus terminal to my hostel.

There is no type of worry quite like the one you feel when your card malfunctions in a foreign country. I'm not going to blast my riches (all $50 worth of it), but I knew I would have a $200 deposit coming into my account.

With no ATM in sight to check my balance and no Wi-Fi around to try to check online, I was, how do the kids say it? SCREWED.

I had saved the route on my GPS beforehand and saw that I could possibly opt for the three-hour trek to my hostel, which would probably turn into five or six hours after you factor in the amount of wrong turns I'd inevitably take.

I scanned the room for kind faces to see if I could perhaps explain my situation to a fellow American who surely has gone through this before. Somehow buy them a drink later on or something.

I look to my left and see scammers trying to sell fake train tickets to a slew of Asian travelers just arriving from their terminal.

I look to my right and see a train approaching and people getting ready to board.

It's my train. The one I needed to take to get to my hostel. Shoot. Think fast.

I hesitantly started making my way toward the doors, eyeballing the ends, looking for "official-looking" people who might be ticket officers.

I see nothing but normal-looking Germans, backpackers, and a risk I couldn't say no to.

I was tired from the long drive in, I was hungry, and if all else failed, I was willing and ready to play the "Stupid American" card.

The "Stupid American" card can be quite handy if you sell it properly.

It's the idea that you're just another clueless American, fresh into this new European continent without the slightest clue of how to operate outside of mommy and daddy's reach.

It's quite pathetic to be honest, but I've seen it work. Over and over again. I swore I'd never be that person.

Yet here I am.

I inched my way onto the train cart and found a little corner where I could prop my suitcase up against the wall. I tried my best to blend in, but my chameleon powers failed me.

I felt some eyes on me, so I kept my head down and started tracking the route on my offline GPS.

With every stop, I grew more and more anxious. I started playing out scenarios where these tall, brawny, scary-looking Germans in bright yellow uniforms (my imagination is too colorful for its own good) would bust in on the doors, each officer assigned to a person, standing in between them and the exit, making sure there was no way they'd get off without showing they paid their fare.

One thing I've come to learn about Germany is that they are efficient. They like their rules and they quite enjoy following them, too.

By that point, I was only two stops away from my hostel and probably one away from getting deported. I feared Germany; I'm not going to lie. I felt like if I were to ever end up in jail abroad, it'd be in a country like Germany, for a reason like not paying a train fare.

I tried to subdue my inner-criminal ways when I saw my stop come. And it took everything in me not to burst through those doors of freedom. There were signs that said this "crime" was punishable by up to 40 euro (45 USD), but I've heard of stories where people were fined 400 euro (450 USD) depending on who catches you.

These ticket controllers are often said to be in their mid-twenties and casually dressed to blend in with everyone else, so they can be pretty hard to spot. Most of my German friends say they've only ever had their tickets checked twice a year. So that was at least reassuring.

The Germans use the honor system and my dishonorable ways gave me one of the biggest scares I ever had abroad. This was the first country I'd been to where public transportation wasn't regulated. This was also the first country where I even considered trying to bypass it.

I have no problem paying for public transport, as they're providing a service I need, but I was stuck between a rock and Donald Trump's head.

It was now 5:30PM and I hadn't eaten anything all day. But to be honest, on a scale of the things I had going for me, I'd say avoiding the fine topped out the need for food at that moment.

After a few wrong turns, which is pretty standard for me, and I've gotten in the habit of factoring in an extra 30 minutes to an hour of ILT (inevitable lost time) when going somewhere on my own, I finally made my way down the right street where I saw the blue dot on my GPS getting bigger showing I was just within meters of the hostel.

I finally checked in on my prepaid booking and made my way to my room exhausted, weak, and hungry.

I plopped into my top bunk, which was reasonably comfortable (but it was the top, so I still hated life), and logged into the Wi-Fi to see what the deal was with my account.

And apparently, my money was still stuck in my PayPal account and hadn't yet been released to my card because I hadn't yet verified my bank account, which I was now approximately 1,200 miles away from. Oh, boy.

I scattered my things in a massive pile on my bed sorting through random paperwork I brought that dealt with anything bank, insurance, or blog-related and Praise God Almighty I found my online banking information and was able to log in, see PayPal's verification code, and enter it directly into the system for them to start releasing the funds into my account.

And then I remembered it would take two to three business days to get deposited. It was a Friday. Meaning the process would start on Monday and arrive in my account at latest by Wednesday.

SUGARBUNNIES AND FUDGECAKES.

But at least the money was on its way, I tried to convince myself. Staying positive, I focused my mind on the good of at least arriving, and decided to freshen up, meet some people downstairs, and maybe go explore the city a bit.

It was still fairly bright outside as I made my way down Berlin's Hackescher Markt (yes, without the 'e') and I was quickly reminded how bad of an idea that was. The area was gorgeous, street music was livening up the atmosphere, and every single corner I turned, there was food. And people. Consuming it happily.

The smells were so strong and penetrated my nostrils hard enough to impregnate my senses and birth a sixth one.

All of a sudden, I was reminded of my hunger and how awful this feeling was. And how vulnerable I became. And how lonely I felt. How miserable this day had been.

For the first time in my two-and-a-half years of traveling, I felt hopeless and alone.

I knew no one in that city except one friend who was preoccupied and pretty far away. And even then, I was too embarrassed to ask her for help as she was probably just scraping by herself.

She also recently became a full-time traveler, and oh what I would've given for just a brief moment of human contact. From a friend, not a stranger. Someone whom I'd known and would treat me as just another person and not the well-known travel blogger I was becoming. I needed a hug. A shoulder. A friend.

I was only a week into this gig and I already longed for a sense of normality and belonging. God help me.

With every step I took, I felt myself getting weaker and my body succumbing to the natural effects of what happens when you don't give it proper nutrition—or any at all, for that matter.

And that is the extent of the sightseeing I was able to do in Berlin.

I turned around and started heading back to the hostel, trying not to breathe in the smells around me, head hanging lower than it ever had, and feeling pretty invisible.

I arrived back in time to be greeted by what looked like a crowd of 50-60 Australians who were in full-blown party mode. They were all having drinks and socializing in the bar by the lobby, and I forced myself not to look too hard as I hurried past them into the elevator and up to my floor.

I convinced myself they would all get miserably drunk and have terrible hangovers the next morning to help get over the fact that I had no money to join them.

It was only 8PM, but I found myself in my pajamas and getting ready for bed as the only thing that could take my mind off my hunger was sleeping. And dreaming. Dreaming of food and happier times when I was a responsible adult and always managed my funds accordingly. Good times, they were.

The first round of sleep lasted a solid five hours until I was awakened by chatty roommates who came back to the room to freshen up before heading back downstairs to pour future hangover liquid into their bodies. You can tell I wasn't bitter about not being there at all.

It took a few seconds of being awake for my stomach to curse at me in the sounds of more growling. I shifted to the other side and think that maybe there's fat somewhere in my stomach that can rotate to another side and confuse my body into thinking there was new food in there.

Can you tell I was great at science growing up? This seemed logical and kind of worked, as I was able to fall asleep again into a seven-hour slumber.

As I was in Berlin as part of a sponsored tour, I woke up the next morning and started getting ready, thinking the bus would depart a little before checkout time.

I took my time showering, getting ready, and tidying up as I assumed I'd be one of the first on the bus.

I get down right about 9AM sharp and look for the tour leaders and other passengers. I see no one.

In a slight panic, I ask the receptionist about the tour company, wondering if they were all still sleeping, because there's no way they'd be gone already, right?!

She nonchalantly informs me that they'd just left about half an hour ago.

"UHHM, EXCUSE ME!?!?! I was supposed to be on that bus!" I explain, feeling the tears of regret building up.

I'm sure this happens on a regular basis, because she then pulled up other bus companies that ran routes to Prague, where I told her I was supposed to be headed next.

This was my first tour with this company, so I was still learning how things went. I had no idea that those same people at the bar until 3AM would somehow be waking up and ready to leave by 8AM in a matter of hours!

Partying truly is a skill set, one that never quite made it to my resumé during my stay in Berlin.

I had a mini meltdown about how I'd just screwed up my first sponsored gig as a full-time travel blogger before realizing my tears wouldn't help with a solution.

I remember a friend from college, Ashley Payne, telling me about one of the budget bus companies that were really popular in Berlin that ran several routes around this region of Europe.

I rushed to check the schedules and timetables and the cheapest one would be in another six hours.

My heart rate starts defaulting back to regular-anxious speed as opposed to overly anxious speed, and I brilliantly remembered that I left a few dollars in my PayPal account instead of transferring everything to my bank account, and I was able to use that to book the bus ticket!

Had I withdrawn everything into my bank account, not only would it be lost in untouchable bank space, unavailable for usage until next Wednesday, but I wouldn't have been able to book that ticket! God is so good and it was just a small glistening moment like that one to help me realize that He's always got my back despite my several lapses in adulthood.

As I was now left with a six-hour wait in the lobby and no longer had access to my room since I checked out, I decided to use this time to work.

I whipped out my laptop and set up my little office in the lobby with the perfect little ray of sunshine coming through to start another beautiful day.

I opened up WordPress, only to have the sounds of my growling stomach overpower my brain's capability to think.

I. Was. Starving. Of course my body wouldn't let me forget.

I was now crossing into Hour #36 of no food, my range of emotions just from that morning had sent my body into more of a panic as I started to feel my hands trembling from weakness as I tried to type.

I glanced around and saw across the hall a jug of fresh water. HOO-RAH!

There seemed to be a breakfast station going on, but the water and coffee looked as free as ever.

I made my way over and drank all the water humanly possible to hold my stomach over for a few more hours.

The bathroom runs were plentiful, but those short savory moments of fresh, new liquid making its way down my throat ("that's what she said," sorry, had to) were enough to keep me satisfied.

Never had I cherished water more than that moment. Never had I truly appreciated its wonderful flavorless goodness that could replenish my soul in just moments.

I was whole again.

Before I knew it, it was time to head over to the bus terminal and make my way on that scary, risky, 30-minute train ride again. Ticketless, and fearing for my life, because Germany.

I tried to use music and headphones to take my mind off the fact that this ride could either be the best or worst ride of my life depending on my fate.

Even with my favorite tunes blasting, I found myself glancing up at every stop, nervously looking out for signs of people who looked like they carried any type of authority or ego.

I saw a couple homeless people board, and for a few moments I felt safe in their presence.

Surely they were spending the little change they had on food and not train fares, so I knew they probably didn't have a ticket, either. So at least my new homeless friends and I would be going together.

I carried on.

One more stop to go. I could feel the freedom again. It was so close.

After what felt like an eternity, I arrive, all smiles, not a thought of my hunger anywhere to be found, and made my way to my terminal.

I was about 45 minutes early, because even after factoring in my ILT (inevitably lost time), I knew there was still room for delays (read: jail time), so I figured it wouldn't hurt.

I'm one of three people waiting underneath our sign, which I hoped to be the correct one according to my e-ticket. Everyone around me looked foreign, so I kept to myself and adhered to the universal "small talk is for weirdos" rule.

A few minutes later, a friendly face and the sign of someone who appeared to speak English propped up beside me.

I shyly turned and asked if he was by chance heading to Prague, making sure I'm under the right sign as I wouldn't put it past myself to screw up another basic task.

A very chipper American accent greeted me with a loud, "YUP!!!"

"Oh! OK, thanks! Wow, I thought you were Dutch or something?" I shamelessly replied.

He laughed, probably unsure of how to respond, but then told me he got that reaction a lot.

I studied his blonde curls, green eyes, and very pale skin, still trying to convince myself he was from Scandinavia, but alas, full-blown Yank. Ha.

Michael Maves was his name. From Portland, Oregon, an economics and political science major from the University of Washington who was currently on a one-way ticket to anywhere.

Like so many other travelers I'd met, he wanted to find more in life and seek happiness through other gains outside of the financial ones America tricks us into believing are all that mattered.

I had never been happier to see or meet another American. Truth be told, I usually avoid them abroad, because it's not a secret we tend to make some of the worst kinds of tourists.

We can be loud, obnoxious, and pretentious to a degree—and this is just talking about me! Ha, but in all seriousness, the reason you travel is to meet other cultures. So it's not that I didn't like mingling with my kind; I just found myself having more open-minded and intellectual conversations with people from other backgrounds.

A few minutes later, our coach arrived. Coach is just what they call buses in Europe, and I felt fancier using that despite my peasant ways.

I was one of the first to board and I was absolutely blown away by the cleanliness, comfort, and space provided on this double-decker machine.

Having overcome my "too cool for school" ways, I made my way toward the front on the lower deck where there was a table and outlets to charge up all my money-making machines (laptop, iPad, cameras, phone). I was in heaven.

I saw everyone making their way to the top deck and I'm thinking PERFECT, because I'll be able to get more work done in peace and quiet.

Shortly after, two slightly drunk Australians made their way to the table parallel to mine. Annoyed at first, but always cordial, I greeted them with a smile and short introductions followed.

They were proper Aussies in the sense that every stereotype I'd seen in Australian media was embodied in these hilarious men.

In their early 20s, they were just like many others, who were on a semi-endless holiday (vacation) around Europe before returning to their jobs back home.

And then my new friend Michael made his way down and asked if he could sit opposite me at my table.

I of course oblige, although I knew that meant no work was going to get done, because I could tell he wanted to talk.

I politely closed my laptop, realizing it's kind of rude to be in a group of four people talking while being antisocial in my corner working. Peer pressure sucks.

I joined in on the very colorful and descriptive conversations as we set off on this eight-hour journey south to the Czech Republic.

We all shared our best travel stories and even one from the large, 6'5" Aussie who talked about working with kids with disabilities on a cruise ship and how he never thought he'd ever be asked to explain what a sunset looked like to a blind girl. It melted his heart and changed the way he saw life and his privileges.

Thank God I put my laptop away. I live for these kind of stories.

As suspicion grew around my job as a travel blogger, I tried to explain what it is I did, or try to do exactly. I also explained how I missed my bus with the company that morning but how it was a blessing in disguise because that afternoon on this luxurious coach with these three guys made it worth it.

Of course comments of "I want your life!" ensue, to which I try to humbly shut down as my growling stomach reminds me of my situation. I NEEDED FOOD.

Michael said he was an aspiring travel blogger himself, so he had a few questions for me that I was more than happy to answer.

We were about a couple hours out from Prague and it's crazy how quick that ride went just because I was around such amazing and entertaining company.

Aussies, by the way, are some of the most hilarious and quick-witted people on this planet. If you need ab workouts, get you an Australian friend. They are GOLDEN. Often drunk, but golden.

We start asking each other where everyone is staying and our plans for the night.

I couldn't help but share how awful this morning had started but how excited I was to just be getting there and having a way to, especially given my "lucky" card situation. I felt myself getting delirious and weak again, given my state.

I ended up telling Michael about my nightmare experience and I'm sure out of pity, which isn't what I wanted, he invited me to dinner.

A little embarrassed, I didn't accept right away, because I didn't want him to think that's why I shared the story. I was just genuinely happy to be in Prague, and I was just a few days away from having the funds in my account anyway.

I temporarily forgot about my hunger as the dominating emotions were relief and joy.

But he insisted. At least in exchange for getting to pick my brain a bit more about travel blogging. That made it sound more fair, so I said yes.

Upon exiting the bus, I felt my natural grin coming out for the first time that day. Life was perfect again. I was in a new country, a new city, and I was just a decent-looking restaurant away from having food in my belly again. Hour #47 had passed and I couldn't believe my body's strength.

We walked around for a few minutes. Several minutes. And I shouldn't have gotten excited too early because my stomach and mind were growing impatient.

"Pleaaaaase stop," I tell myself. Mainly, my stomach. It was turning and aching for something and didn't like the fact that my mind told it food was coming prematurely.

Michael only had a credit card on him because he too had some issues with getting his camera and debit card stolen recently.

So we had to first find a place that was willing to take cards in Prague—which of course, is not many.

When we finally found one, I propped my suitcase up and we awaited the menus. Well, he did I'm sure. I was just anxious for whatever complimentary bread they would bring out.

How do I not act like this was my first meal in two days when this was my first meal in two days? I apologized in advance for my barbaric ways and dug in when the tray of pita bread came out.

I. Was. In. Heaven.

Pita Heaven, to be exact. By the way, Pita Heaven has beer. And it was magical.

We toasted to us both being in this new city and country at the same time and just the off-chance that we even ended up meeting due to a disaster on my end.

To this day, we're still great friends and reunited in Bangkok last October, where he was living for a bit, and then again this year in July at the Tomorrowland Music Festival in Belgium. Love ya, Mike!

Ironically, Prague turned out to be my least favorite city, which you remember reading about in chapter 2.7. But despite that hellacious experience, I still would love to return someday for a second opinion.

After Prague, I was off on a few more stops over the next nine days where I finished in Munich, Germany, and gained a new sense of empathy.

I made my usual bakery run for my daily bread and butter, and I saw a homeless man with a hungry sign.

This wasn't new to me. I knew there were hungry people everywhere. But never in my life had I felt more convicted, because I remembered what I went through in Berlin.

Never in my life did I ever have to worry about where my next meal would come from. I was humbled to a degree I never knew existed.

I'd been hungry before in the past. You know, when you're at a restaurant and every waiter heading your way ends up passing you up, and you're all like, "I'm sooooo hungry!" Yeah, that was the prior extent of my "hungry."

So I knew hungry. But I didn't know starving. I didn't know 21,000 people die every day due to hunger or hunger-related causes (source: poverty.com).

That's one person every four seconds.

Humble pie. I'll have a slice to go, please.

I went back in the bakery and bought this man a large sandwich and drink.

No, it won't solve the hunger problem around the world. And yes, he will eventually get hungry again. But if I could just brighten his day and temporarily solve his worries for a brief moment in time just like Michael did for me, I've done my job to better humanity.

People think we need these large platforms and solutions to rid the world of its bad all at once.

Yet there are so many baby steps and little things we could be doing within our own community that could affect people on a larger scale.

What was one of the most awful and humiliating phases of my travels turned into the most inspiring and memorable.

I have never shared this story on social media because it was just too personal to me. I was embarrassed and vulnerable, but I share it here because it's a message that ties in so well with my story on a spectrum of all the good and bad that can happen when you set off on an indefinite adventure.

And even when something starts off as a nightmare experience, there's usually a lesson or reward at the end of it. I'm so thankful for both.

"How I Legally Travel Around Europe Without Needing A Visa"

As every country has its own set of rules and regulations, this is only specifically directed toward North Americans, as I can only speak from my own experience. It's also pretty hard to keep track of regularly changing laws and rules, so please take this as a guideline and not a blueprint.

I first traveled to Europe by way of London, with a six-month visa to work at Harlaxton College in the UK, the institution where I studied abroad back in 2012. To work abroad in Europe, you do need a visa, but to travel abroad, you don't.

So even if that weren't the case, know that North Americans are allowed to legally visit and stay in the UK for up to six months. However, you aren't allowed to work or have access to public funds.

This would be a good chance to get your foot in the door, network, travel locally, and plan your next steps to find a permanent way of living abroad.

When I booked a one-way ticket to London, it was because I knew I would try to prolong my stay indefinitely.

I was only allowed to stay up to eight months in London before I'd have to leave the country, and I never occupied my mind too hard with what would come after until about 10 days before my contract was up.

Desperation was settling in and Google became my friend. I learned about this beautiful thing called the Schengen Area. It's a part of Europe comprised of 26 European countries who've all settled an agreement to have a virtually borderless system. So someone like me, who owned an American passport, was free to travel to any of these 26 countries without needing a visa, to stay and live legally for up to 90 days within an 180-day time frame.

So essentially it's three months in, three months out.

And while in these countries, you could supplement income with local jobs such as private English teaching, au-pairing, translating, bartending, hostel work, and sports clubs. All of which I did at one point or another.

So let's say you want to live in Spain and travel around Europe like I did. You could stay in Spain and have your home base to store all your things while still having the freedom to travel around Europe very cheaply and lightly.

On any given day, I could find flights to Paris for $20 or buses to Italy for just under $50. Whatever mode of transportation you preferred, Spain was a perfect hub to do so. Ridesharing networks such as Blablacar also proved to be incredibly useful as I once found myself paying $10 to get picked up from my hostel in Paris and dropped off in Amsterdam. Ten bucks, guys! That's the cost of two coffees these days!

When I talk about affordable travel, it's not to shame those who don't want to prioritize it as a part of their life. Not everybody is made to travel or desires to, and that's fine! But when I discover all these cheap resources and networks that allow debt-prone college graduates like me to see the world on nickels and dimes, how could I not get excited about it and share!?

Not to mention, when putting it in perspective to the things we shelve out hundreds for anyway (concert tickets, sporting games, shoes, jewelry, etc.), it really does come down to prioritization.

A reader once sternly asked me why I don't write about traveling with kids. Well, ma'am...unless I dress up a pillow and pretend it's a baby, I have no idea what that's like! I'm childless! Sorry for this crime, but I can only write and share about my experiences. And that's not to discriminate, but it's the only thing I know.

There are hundreds of travel bloggers out there who each cater to their unique markets and niches. Traveling with kids, with spouses, with pets, with disabilities, with allergies, you name it!

And if you can't find one, then be the first! *ding ding* There's your business idea!

It's also worth mentioning that the Schengen visa is nothing more than a stamp in your passport upon arrival in your first Schengen country.

There are also countries that are a part of the European Union but aren't a part of the Schengen Agreement. It makes it slightly complicated but also convenient in case you need somewhere to wait on your count to reset in a country such as Romania, Croatia, or Montenegro—all incredibly cheap, friendly, and affordable destinations as I've camped out for extended amounts of time in all three.

As of 2016, these are the countries that are a part of the Schengen Agreement:

- Austria
- Belgium
- Czech Republic
- Denmark
- Estonia
- Finland
- France
- Germany
- Greece
- Hungary
- Iceland (not a European Union Member State)
- Italy

- Latvia
- Liechtenstein (not a European Union Member State)
- Lithuania
- Luxembourg
- Malta
- Netherlands
- Norway (not a European Union Member State)
- Poland
- Portugal
- Slovakia
- Slovenia
- Spain
- Sweden
- Switzerland (not a European Union Member State)

So for someone who wants to live and travel in Europe extensively, three months is a great start to get your foot in the door, find a home base, or at least somewhere you can store your things, then pack a light backpack and travel around.

You can pick up small gigs on the road like the jobs I mentioned in the earlier chapter, or if you've saved enough to not need to work, simply enjoy the fruits of your labor and relish in your Schengen freedom.

As you may have noticed, the United Kingdom is not in the Schengen Agreement, so if you wanted to reset your count there, remember you're allowed to be in the UK for up to six months as a tourist! Pretty great! Again, this varies based on your native country, so please refer to your country's embassy guidelines for specifications regarding your passport.

So given this information, you could potentially live in and around Europe as long as you wanted, visa and illegal-boyfriend-free! #GOALS2K16

PART THREE

The Adventure!

"The 10 Big No-Nos Of Travel"

As a solo traveler a majority of the time, I've become very observant. I take note of my surroundings and people's energy constantly, because it helps keep me safe and aware.

It doesn't matter who you are or where you're from, there are ten sure ways to piss off locals in any country, regardless of their background, if you adhere to the following:

---

1 — Dressing Provocatively

I'm not here to monitor your wardrobe or try to control how you should feel about what you want to show off to strangers. I will say, however, that it's not only disrespectful to assume every country is okay with half of your butt cheeks hanging below your ripped jean shorts (why is this still a thing?!), but that it will bring you (more) unwanted attention.

And depending on where you are, no matter how unfair, men will look at it as an invitation. If you travel solo, you need to go the extra mile in maintaining a wardrobe that you not only feel comfortable in, but that respects the environment of the country you're visiting.

2 — *Walking In A Line Of More Than Three People On Small Sidewalks*

In small villages, in Europe in particular, sidewalks can be extremely narrow. We know you want to stop and snap photos of every waking thing around you because it adds to the foreign element of you being abroad, even if it's something like dog poop on the ground. Doesn't matter, it's Spanish dog poop! Therefore, snap, snap!

Locals who are just making their daily commute back home or to the local market don't want to wait every five seconds behind you. Try to be aware of people around you, especially as you make abrupt stops every few seconds for photos.

3 — *Ignoring Bike Lanes*

Bikes are a religion for bikers in bike-heavy cities such as Amsterdam and Salzburg. If you do so much as to walk in the bike lanes, expect to get dinged at and politely pushed over if you don't move quickly enough.

Bikers can be ruthless because of the amount of times they have to remind people that the bike picture you're standing on is because about 20-something bikes will be passing that very mark every minute. Stay in your (pedestrian) lane, folks!

4 — *Using Your Outdoor Voice On The Metro*

Ohhh, Americans. You'll see 'em, smell 'em, and hear 'em a mile away coming from their last Metro connection.

I don't know why we have such loud and obnoxious tones when in private and quiet settings, but I've heard girls recounting their last-night hook-ups and guys spilling details of where they'll get their drugs.

It's just unnecessary. Enjoy your time, have fun, but be respectful of the commute that most locals will be making and have been making for the last 10 years in peace and quiet.

5 — *Comparing Your Home Country To The One You're In*

Piggybacking off the last point, why do people feel the need to go on a vacation if they're going to do nothing but compare how much better things are where they're from?

It's one thing to take note of your privileges being from a First World country, but to openly discuss your hatred or distaste for another country's customs or traditions, especially on a place like the Metro where there's guaranteed to be at least one English-speaking local within ear's distance...just stop. Stop talking altogether.

6 — *Ignoring Street Signs*

Especially in countries such as Germany where I've seen people get scolded by older locals for crossing when the pedestrian sign is red, try to respect your environment and don't use your pedestrian's right of way as your right to be a douchebag.

In Barcelona, they will give you a polite tap with their car to remind you they don't care and will run you over next time. It's sometimes funny. Just don't be that guy.

7 — *Not Knowing How To Handle Your Liquor*

This is quite obvious and something that's widespread, although I'm going to single out Americans, Brits, and Australians for having some of the most barbaric and belligerent behavior I've seen while abroad when it comes to bars and pubs.

Unnecessary fights started, vomit everywhere, and stereotypes reinforced. Guys, you're on vacation, I get it. But do yourself a favor and keep your embarrassing lack of self-control in your home country. It's such a shame to see that girl or guy being dragged out of a club, barely able to stand, vomit all over their clothes, or just looking lifeless. Have fun, but have a brain. too. They go well together.

---

8 — *Standing On The Left Side Of Escalators*

This is pretty standard all over Europe, but please for the love of all things right in the world, do NOT stand on the left side of escalators. Stand on the right. The left is for people in a hurry who can speed up their time by walking up them.

If you fail to adapt to this very common and basic unspoken rule, you'll be met with stern faces, hard taps on your shoulder, or even shoves. Just be mindful that the city you're vacationing in is other people's everyday home, and they have places to be that don't involve museums and nightclubs.

---

9 — *Not Trying To Learn Greetings Of The Local Language*

No matter how long you're staying in a place or how immersed you want to be in the culture, the very simple task of learning how to say "Hi," "Please," and "Thank you" will get you further than you know.

Not only is it slightly rude to assume and expect every country you visit to know a second or third language that conveniently caters to yours, but you ought to take the extra step in showing that you respect and appreciate being in their presence and it's the easiest way to get strangers to help you out.

---

10 — Overplanning

Nothing is more anticlimactic about a trip than when you overplan every detail of it. I understand you want to try to check off every museum, attraction, and photo op to fulfill this faux sensation that you did everything possible in the mere 24 hours you allocated for this city; I get it.

But what you miss out on are the spontaneous adventures, organic friendships, and authentic experiences.

While you're too busy trying to curate a perfect photo sequence of pictures from the day, you're missing out on the sunsets, the transits, and the random encounters you could have with locals.

I've stopped researching things to do in a city before I arrived, and instead, I plan on meeting up with locals and asking them in person what they love about their city first. Hearing suggestions from someone who's lived there all their lives and me, not having concrete plans, I can easily adjust my schedule accordingly. There's so much liberation in that!

"The Best & Worst Travel Companions"

So you've finally pulled the trigger. You've picked a country. You've set the dates. And you've told your boss that you're [never coming back] and ready to use your vacation days from work.

Now, the hard part. Whom do you go with?

As an advocate of traveling solo, I know this type of crazed sorcery isn't for everyone, and if this is your first trip abroad, you should definitely bring someone with you. And I can't say I speak from experience from this entire list, but I've definitely seen, heard, and been the third wheel to these type of people on trips, and I promise you, you'll save yourself the headache and regret of bringing them if you choose wisely in advance and take all this into account!

Disclaimer: This isn't to say that you should never go anywhere with this type of people, but if you're planning the trip of a lifetime to a place you've been dying to visit, in order to maximize the good times, the person you're bringing along will be crucial. And everyone knows at least one of these types of people. And if you can't think of anyone who fits the list, perhaps it is you. Meep. Awk. Don't shoot the messenger.

1 — *The High-Maintenance Person*

If you're a seasoned traveler, you know there's a lot of unsexy aspects of travel that us nomads don't always broadcast or share. You're sleeping on airport floors to catch red-eye flights, packing yourself like sardines on unsanitary Metros, and sharing your precious oxygen with strangers everywhere...the nerve of such a life! Ha.

But the last thing you need or want is someone reminding you how uncomfortable they are or how "in America" they never had to worry about x, y, and z. These people probably make great fashion stylists and know all the hot spots for the weekend, but leave them at home and take someone who knows how to let their hair down without worrying about a couple tangled strands in the process.

---

2 — *The Filthy Rich Person*

So, true story guys...there was a D-list celebrity gal that I met through mutual contacts who was coming to visit Barcelona and wanted to hang out for a couple days. Of course I was more than happy to show her around like I do with anyone who reaches out, but her conversations kept directing back to luxury hotels and 5-star lounges to peruse. "You know you can't be hangin' round no 5-star lounges with a 2-star budget!" I kept telling myself.

I'm at a different point in my life where I don't need or desire fancy things like that. So if you're bringing someone along who doesn't have a limit to their credit card, the pressure is on you to casually match their spending habits.

She asked to eat on the rooftop of a prestigious hotel with entrees starting in triple-digit prices...meanwhile I'd normally still be living off the cookies I managed to smuggle through the airport two days prior. Let's just say I flaked and caught a very bad, uhh...flu. I'm just not about to pay a car note price for food that will end up in the toilet a few hours later.

LEFT: Paros Island, Greece
by Mary Beth Photography

SUBSEQUENT QUOTE PAGES:

1 — Bucharest, Romania

2 — Nice, France

3 — Wadi Rum Desert, Jordan

BELOW: Ibiza, Spain

*Life abroad is every bit
what you make of it.
And I choose to make
this life nothing short of
extraordinary.*

*Travel has opened my
heart to crave a way of
life I never knew I had
an appetite for.*

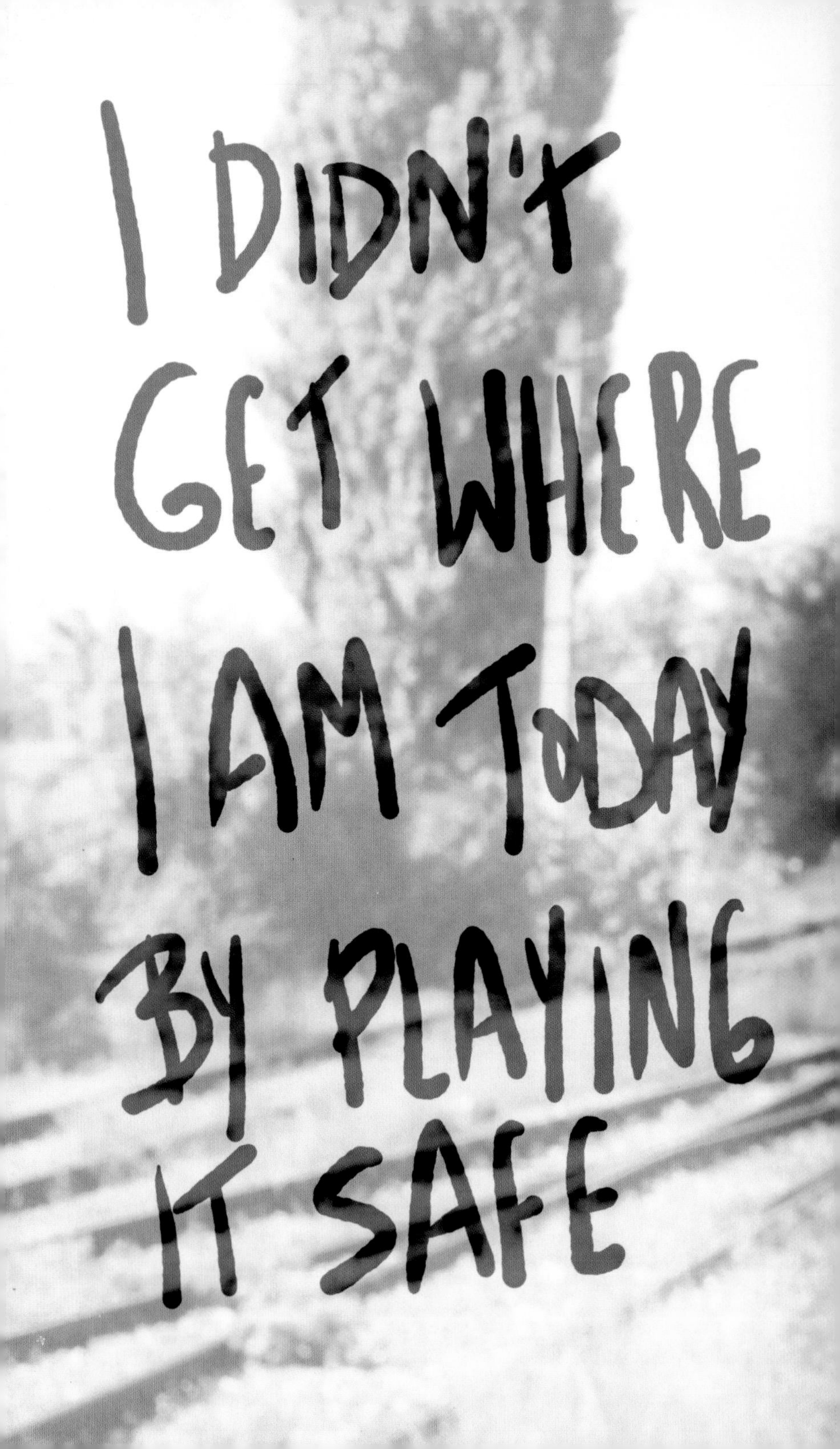
I DIDN'T
GET WHERE
I AM TODAY
BY PLAYING
IT SAFE

or following rules + conforming to the shape others molded for my life

If you want something bad enough, *** NO $$$ dollar amount will come in the way of THAT.

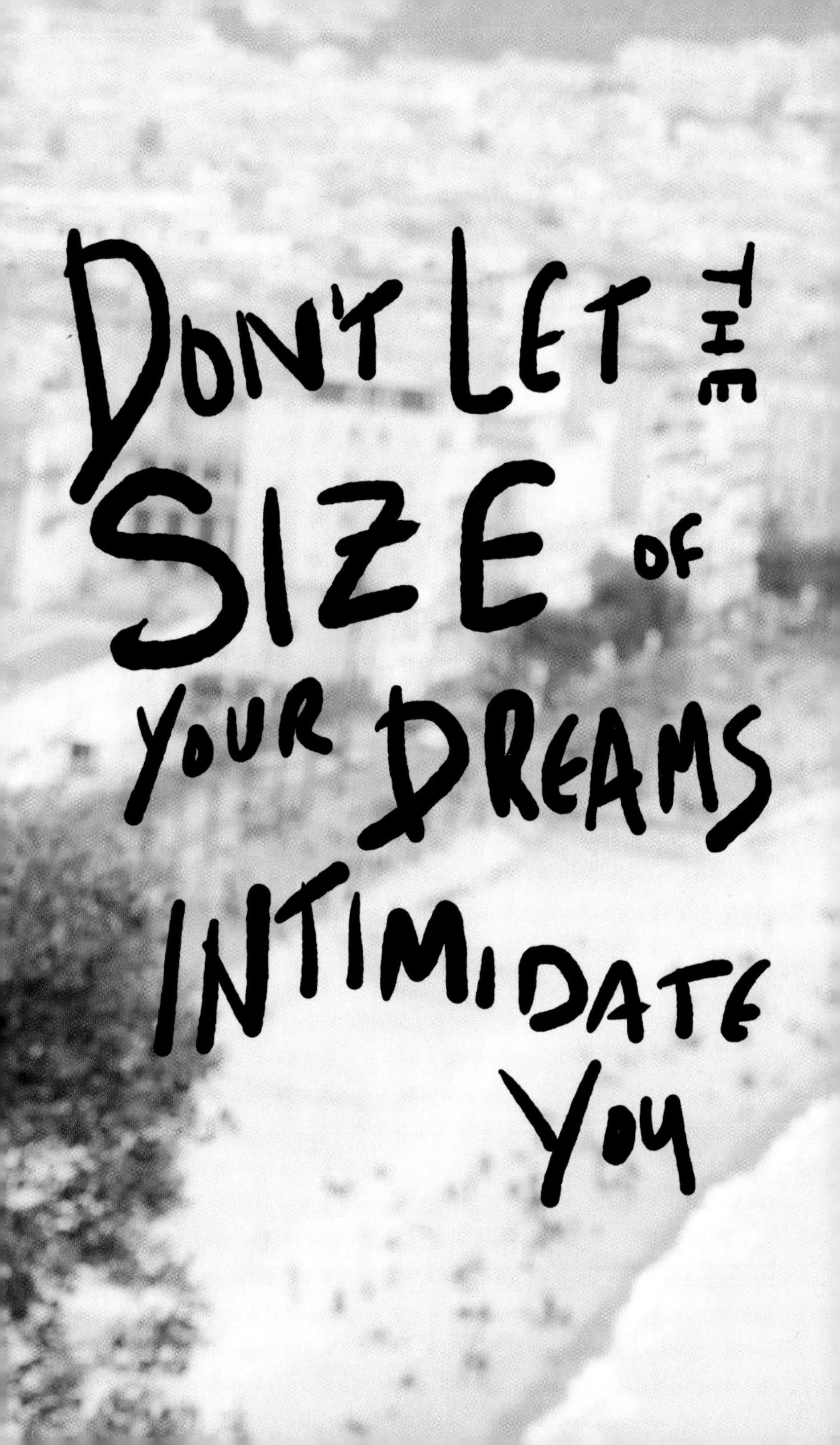
DON'T LET THE
SIZE OF
YOUR DREAMS
INTIMIDATE
YOU

Life gives you
Two things to be
happy about —
THE DAY
YOU WERE
BORN +

THE DAY
YOU
FIGURED
OUT
WHY.

TOP: Island of Burano,
Venice, Italy

RIGHT: Athens, Greece

*Surround yourself with
people who challenge
you, encourage you, but
most of all, inspire you
to tap into the potential
of greatness you were
destined for.*

*Everyone has a special
gift they can contribute
to making this world a
better place, and your gift
may or may not be a solo
trip away from discovery.*

3 — *The New Boyfriend/Girlfriend*

Okay, so I get it. I really do. You're head over heels and you want to start creating new and exciting memories together...so what better way than to travel? But in the butterfly phase, before you've even had your first argument, a foreign country where neither of you speak the local language isn't the most relaxing environment to hash out your differences or argue over where to eat dinner, because we all know that argument is inevitable.

Not only will you both be out of your elements, but you'll notice things about them that will irritate you more than ever. You guys will bicker over the smallest things and you'll be doing it in a beautiful foreign destination where your memories will become tainted with arguments over spilled milk. Traveling together should be the next phase of your relationship...after you guys have gone through the emotions of wanting to strangle each other in your home country first.

4 — *Single Sally*

Can we all agree that we know exactly the kind of girls I'm talking about without feeling like this is a slut-shaming session? I understand someone else's body count is none of my business, but when they're the reason you're locked out of your hotel room or stranded in the middle of nowhere, then yeah...it's kinda your business now.

It's no secret that there are people who travel abroad with the sole purpose of finding a spouse and meanwhile testing several potential suitors along the way. Not only does it put your third-wheelin' self in an awkward position, but it'll ruin your friendship with this person and subsequently, the entire trip as well. Only good wingwomen allowed.

Part of knowing whom you can travel with is also knowing who can handle their liquor and behavior when their tolerance is in question. I think it's obvious Americans get a bad reputation abroad for not being able to drink responsibly due to the differences in the legal drinking age.

So some Americans come to Europe with that liberated feeling of being able to purchase and drink all their newly legal heart desires and normally, this is broadcasted for others to judge accordingly all over the pavement outside the pub entrance.

Not only is your night spent holding your friend's hair over the toilet, but now Hungover Hannah can't get out of bed at all the next day and you feel obligated to stay and remind her how she wasn't barfing to the melody of Chewbacca last night and look after her. One and a half days of your trip now wasted.

But oh, alas...the day has come where Lazarus emerges from his or her tomb, and despite her pleas to do better and make up for the other night, you find yourself again cleaning vomit out of her hair, apologizing to the bouncer, mayor, and all others she mocked in the process, while swimming through tears of regret in all their salty glory.

If you can avoid bringing any of these five types of people on your dream getaway, I promise your vacation will be even more amazing the minute you step off that plane.

So now that we've awkwardly acknowledged the types of people you should avoid traveling with, it's time to appreciate and shout out the type of people who will take a normal trip and make it an experience of a lifetime.

Hopefully you each have a person in your life that you can refer to from the categories I mention below.

1 — *The Resourceful Person*

Before you've even arrived, this person will have downloaded the top five apps that will not only navigate you through the most confusing and remote parts of town, but you'll be able to translate every foreign word with the flash of a screen and be going to local events that they found through an online network of travelers.

That person for me is Kristin Eberman, my former boss in the UK. She is one of the most well-traveled people I know, and as traveling is somewhat of a sport, she is definitely at the top of her game. With over 30 countries under her belt, she's done more living than the average American and I will forever keep her as my go-to gal if I'm ever planning a great escape (read: world domination)!

2 — *The Social Butterfly*

This person is great to bring along especially if you consider yourself an introvert and the idea of having to put on pants and deal with people irritates you. Having the opposite type of energy around you to bring out the awesomeness you know you already possess will be golden.

The best part about a social butterfly is they can strike up a conversation with just about anyone and they have a charming way of bringing everyone together. I met Christine Tjhia from Indonesia last year at an Instameet in London and we immediately hit it off. She's the kind of gal who lights up a room with her style, poise, and incredible fashion sense. Social butterflies make your social life just a tad bit more awesome, and they are super photogenic on the inside and out!

A trip isn't a trip unless you've got the pics to prove it. You can tell me you jumped out of a plane and landed 100 feet from an active volcano, but unless I see it on your Instagram, I'm not sure I'm buying your story.

It's 2016, and with the rise of better technology and photo-based social media, it's easier than ever to share Kodak moments of fun events in your life. But when you have someone who's already got the eye for a good shot, you can guarantee a new default profile picture in store.

Pictures truly do speak a thousand words, and if you've got a friend whose companionship comes with this awesome talent, you've hit the jackpot. Some of my best travel photos have been the lucky chance where I meet another professional photographer on the road or when I travel with a fellow blogger who has that keen eye for a good capture.

You could be looking at the same thing, but the photographer will see and capture an angle that the average person would never think of. It's amazing and I love being around that kind of creative energy. My friend Derio Ilari from Argentina was that person for me.

Photographers know how to turn moments into golden memories with the single click of a button. It's like magic. And it's awesome.

4 — The Risk-Taker Or Daredevil

When it comes to the amazing world of travel, sure it's preferable to do everything the safe way. But the way I see it, just be smart enough to have a plan but dumb enough to have some stories.

Because the best travel memories come from those "brilliant" ideas to trespass through unmarked territory or sneaking into the most popular club in town and forgoing the $50 cover fee because, well...peasantry.

Don't get me wrong; I'm not a "rule-breaker" per se, but I take a lot of risks. But at least they're always calculated ones, to make sure the potential consequence would never outweigh the reward. Daredevils, historically, are winners. Nobody gets ahead always playing by the rules (ain't that right, New England Patriots)?

And you have more fun when you don't go by the book. The stories my friend Greg Allan from Canada has of all the times he's cut corners while traveling will have you laughing hard enough to never need to do another ab workout again. Not to mention the fun we had in the skyscraper buildings in London all the way to the beaches of Barcelona. I know if I want to be in for a thrill, I'm calling my Canadian buddy Greg. Every. Single. Time. It's been fun to have traveled together in five countries now, and I'm counting down our reunion for the next!

---

5 — *The Glass Half Full (Of Wine) Person*

In case you didn't already know this, and I hate to be the one to break it to you...but something will go terribly wrong on your trip. Like, I promise you. The chances of this are just upwards of 99.9999%.

But don't fret, because it's more than likely an issue that's completely unforeseen and out of your control. A flight delay, a missed connection, lost luggage, a pickpocket disaster, death by hangover, etc.

When and if any of the former happen, the glass-half-full person will help rid you of any worry and anxiety. Negative Nancies and Pessimistic Peters are the WORST and have no room in my circle and certainly not on my trip.

Everyone loves a person who can see the light in any dark situation, or more relatively speaking, the wine glass is always half-full to them. Stress has no room for you inside your carry-on, so don't let these unwarranted emotions ruin a trip!

I have two friends named Hannah Miller and Hannah Schaake (also Baker University alumnae) who were these people for me when they came to Grantham, England for a staycation while I served as an intern at Harlaxton College.

I'm a lucky gal to have these five types of people in my life and I hope to be traveling with each of them again soon!

"The Worst People To Share A Metro With"

A majority of the population east of the Atlantic Ocean uses public transportation to get around, especially the Metro, which is completely opposite of what I'm used to in America.

So if you're traveling around Europe, get comfortable and used to the idea that the Metro is your best friend. It's super convenient, cheap, and in cities such as London, it's fairly easy to understand.

However, this doesn't mean that everyone can adhere to the 10 unspoken rules of the Metro. These people you will meet over and over again. They suck at life, so make sure you never become these people, either.

The Man-Spreader

The one with balls so big, they need three seats. All right, buddy, I'm going to need you to respect my space, get your knee off of mine, and put your little sacks of nothing where they're not out on display.

Let's have a moment of silence for all the potential children this man could have, should have, but won't because he's the worst type of human being and no woman in her right mind wants to reproduce with people who try to reserve couches for peanuts (all the puns intended).

The Ball-Adjuster

This could even be the same person as the Man-Spreader if you want to talk about hitting the lottery. But not to be confused with his ways, this man at least has the decency to not waste any seats by standing up.

But just like that, all good qualities become voided by the fact he feels the need to adjust himself multiple times on a mere two-minute journey.

To make matters worse, you accidentally (or purposely, I don't judge) make eye contact, and now he wants you to have his babies and you've never contemplated ripping out your uterus and chucking it out the window until that point. I think I would rather have the man-spreader. Or die. Yeah, dying sounds better.

The "Can You Hear My Freedom From All the Way Over There?" American

Sigh. Just in case you forgot the smell of freedom, here comes Yankee Doodle on his pony, reeking of cologne smelling like bacon and guns, waving their American flag loud and proud, and making sure everyone on the cart knows it.

They will toot and boot their reckons and beckons about how America is God's country and the most blessed land in the world. There's also a very strong chance this kind of person will be from Texas. Sorry, not sorry. #truthbombs

The Cop-A-Feel-er

Never mind the fact this Metro is packed like sardines, because the opportunistic cop-a-feel-er will have placed a hand anyway on every butt or hip they can. And by the time you turn around, you're met with ten backs and you have no clue of knowing who did it. It's immature, it's annoying, it's disgusting. And there's a special place in hell for this kind of person. Right next to people who eat hot food on the Metro, which leads me to my next point...

Gourmet Eaters

If I told you that the phone you're simultaneously switching from hand to food has more bacteria on it than a toilet seat, would you carry on? Not to mention, some Metro carts are used for homeless people to sleep in until they're caught. So you can believe that urine and vomit stains over time have seeped into the seats, walls, and poles.

And then when I see you lick your fingers to get the last of that chili dip off you, then grab onto the pole to stand up, I want to vomit. Preferably on you. But life isn't always fair.

My Bag Has a Metro Ticket, Too

I'm not quite sure if this idea is new or not, but newsflash, YOUR PURSE IS NOT A PERSON. Neither is your bag, your suitcase, your dog, or your ego.

I don't get it. When there are elderly people stuck standing by the doors and you're sitting there, manspreading with your backpack on the seat next to you, what planet do you live on, because this one does not revolve around you.

Starers

Eye contact is good at work. It's good in relationships. And it's good when there's a mutual attraction, interaction, or need for both parties to look in each other's direction.

Eye contact is not, however, good for:

— adjusting your manhood
— picking your nose
— eating the boogers from prior item
— after you've farted
— when you're mouthing the lyrics to music only you can hear (you look psychotic; please look elsewhere).

People That Ignore Elderly & Pregnant People

It's unbelievable the lack of empathy some people have when yielding reserved seats to the people they're designated for. From fellow riders going as far as to claim, "It's not my fault you got yourself pregnant" or pretending not to see the elderly man walking toward them, a little part of me crumbles inside.

The seats are even color-coded half the time! If there's limited seating and you see an elderly or pregnant woman walking toward you, there's got to be a point where common courtesy kicks in and you're like, "Oh! Perhaps this is where I practice my human decency as a fellow human and stuff?" Please tell me there is.

The Reeker

This person looks and smells like they've been drinking since George Bush's presidency. The first one!

They reek of poor life choices, cheap hookers, and a six-pack of regret.

They'll make everyone within a one-mile radius of them put up with their non-showering ways.

They usually have no idea where they're going, just kind of killing time and trying to blend in with humanity again. They might spew out some chauvinistic and misogynistic remarks for attention, but just like their smell, we will ignore that, too.

Long live the Metro, and short live these people.

"Secrets To Taking Stunning Travel Photos"

It's hard to live in a culture where vacations and travels are judged by the pictures you share of them. Yes, some can argue that's not always the case...and those are the same people who have albums worth of memories splattered across social media. So there's that. I mean, it's 2016. Pictures tell a thousand words of stories that we hardly do justice for without graphic evidence.

In a perfect world (I'd be married to Channing Tatum), we'd all be able to hire private photographers to follow us everywhere on trips, snapping every candid (read: staged) moment, and making us look like the supermodels we all could be if fast food chains and Nutella didn't exist.

When I go through my emails, one of the most common questions I get asked by readers is who my photographer is, to which I usually answer with Joe Schmoe from Germany or South Africa or Brazil, because it's just the helping hand of strangers everywhere.

Pictures can be direct reflections of our trips because for a moment, we feel like we've frozen time and turned it into this beautifully crafted Instagram-worthy moment that people near and far can gaze at or draw inspiration from.

Even after I listed the many reasons why a photographer makes one of the best travel companions, I still prefer solo travel when it comes to jet-setting, and although there will be awkwardness in the initial approach of finding someone to take your picture, after almost 40 countries and approximately 10,000 extremely awkward encounters, I've figured out a magic formula for this.

As a portrait photographer myself, I'm used to giving direction to others to make the ever-so-awkward experience of someone pointing a hole at your face a little smoother as you stand there hoping to God your pimples took a vacation that day and contemplating which Instagram filter will hide all of your insecurities (Spoiler Alert: none of them). So listen up closely, my non-photogenic lilies.

Take Babies For Ransom

No one is immune to theft while traveling, and if you travel solo, you run the risk of placing your camera into the hands of a thief (looking at you, Barcelona). But there is a foolproof way to make sure the person you're about to approach isn't going to run off with your hundred- to thousand-dollar DSLR.

Speaking of DSLRs, if a person has a DSLR around their neck, chances are they will respect a fellow (expensive-camera-buyer) or photographer and treat it with the same care as they would their own. Not only that, but there's a good chance they already know how to work your camera and you don't have to spend ten minutes explaining how to push a button.

Okay, so if a person has kids with them, specifically a toddler in a stroller, you know for sure they aren't running off. You take my camera sir, and I'll take your baby and put a ransom on that @$#. But don't worry, I don't discriminate. This applies to kids, spouses, and pets as well.

Scratch My Back And I Scratch Yours?

So if you see a couple taking an awkward selfie and you gently offer to take a picture for them, 99% of the time they will automatically reciprocate the offer. This takes the pressure off you having to ask, because they will offer first, and it's also a good chance to scope out how you want your picture to look after you take theirs.

If you try an angle with them that comes out well, you can tell them to look at the picture you took of them and try to imitate the results. People are usually so cute about imitating my squats and angles when I ask, and the results are always exactly what I want. Speaking of...

In Angles We Trust

It's amazing what perspective does to enhancing a photo. Using an angle apart from the "holding my camera directly in front of my face while standing straight" does wonders to the eye and it's like Photoshopping a picture without the expensive software.

To make a person, monument, or subject appear greater than they are in person, crouch down and angle upwards. This also applies to shorter people who want to add some height to their pictures.

When you think of a scenery, think of the thousands, maybe millions who've been on those exact grounds you're standing on... taking the exact same photo, with the exact same standard angle. You want to try to take a picture from an angle that you won't see a replica of on the first page of Google Images because it's so unique.

I've seen enough pictures of Big Ben to feed a Third World country suffering from London deprivation if that were a thing, yet and still, there are some amazing Instagram accounts who remind me of the beauty of a cliché city from the eyes of people who don't capture it in a cliché way. And it's beautiful.

Some different angles include a "Bird's Eye View" which would require you to take a picture of something from the top and see it the way a bird does. This is usually best for Instagramming pictures of food, which I only try doing on special occasions, fancy dining, or immaculately prepared feasts during holidays. Try different things out and get creative!

Posing For The Photo

So you've found your photographer and you've made eye contact with his toddler, in case they want to crawl off as an accomplice to this potential thievery when you're ready to strike a pose.

But how on Earth do you control your face? What do you do with your hands? Is this constipation or is that just your body reminding you how awkward life is? Here to help, kids.

First off, before you get ready for the picture, find a setting that complements you. Patterned backgrounds, bodies of water, and large monuments all make great backdrops and are iconic for "look at me, I traveled" and stuff. And that's the look we're going for. ;)

It also helps to use accessories to keep your hands occupied. The reason I love fedoras is because they hide a percentage of my alien-shaped head and give me something to place my hands on or tinker with if I feel the moment is right.

If you want to appear a bit slimmer, try slanting your torso and hips just a bit to the side, as well as elongating your neck and turning it slightly to an angle, as if giving off a smirk.

All this sounds very robotic, so to combat that, you want to have the person count down the picture and while they're at 3, 2... you'll be looking backwards, down, or in the sky, and then you'll snap your head into place by 1 and the picture will appear a tad bit more natural in all of its staginess.

Also, don't be afraid to ask them to take two or three shots before you review them. Chances are, one will be blurry, one will have your eyes closed, and the third will be gold. Repeat these steps with at least three iconic sceneries and you'll be sure to come back with several favorites and a new default profile picture.

One of the most fun things about being a photographer is directing my clients to do odd things for the sake of a good photo. Odd things include "laughing out loud" on cue, looking at a branch in the tree in front of you, or stroking your hair. These non-candid actions or movements make a picture appear more natural and authentic. Oh, the irony.

But I promise this is THE #1 TRICK TO GET A NATURAL SMILE IN YOUR PICTURE: Don't smile for the picture, actually laugh out loud and you'll be amazed at how much more fun and genuine your smile shines through.

Don't be afraid to be silly! There are some people who go on these amazing trips and don't have one single photo of themselves on the trip, and I find that absolutely absurd. Okay, you don't like taking pictures, maybe. But anybody can grab a picture from Google and say they were there. Being in the picture is not only undeniable proof that you were there, but it conveys so much more. Your mood, your expression, and your body all change daily, and you get a chance to see how all of that looked while on a trip to laugh or gawk at in the future!

Most of all, embrace the moment! You're in gorgeous, foreign territory! Even if it was the crappiest time of your life (which, uhhm...impossible), still make that picture hold thousands of memories you won't be able to adequately retell with words.

For taking sharper images with a nice Bokeh effect, I shoot with a Canon 60D and a 50mm f1/8 lens. If you've held or used this lens before, you can vouch for how easy and lightweight it is. It's the only lens I've shot with in my last two years of travel, and it has an amazingly sharp focus on its subjects. You can get it for about $100 on Amazon and it works great on any DSLR camera body you may have. Note: It's not a zoom lens, so if you're used to stock lenses, this will be a bit of an adjustment and sometimes a challenge to explain to strangers.

So between self-timers and your newfound confidence to approach strangers, I expect your Instagram to be dripping with gorgeousness. ;)

"Your Vibe Attracts Your Tribe"

L ike, like-minded minds. It's so important to meet and surround yourself with people who not only think like you, but think with you as well.

I was in Barcelona back in September 2014 when I was reminded of how essential this is for maintaining a positive and productive mentality.

Her name was Jelisa Moné, a fellow expat who was living in Ibiza, Spain at the time and we had connected through mutual friends (aka Instagram).

I can't tell you what a spark of life she gave me being able to bounce ideas off each other and swap wanderlust stories of what being abroad has done for our lives, and how the change is constant, uncomfortable, and oh-so-rewarding.

It's hard to explain this feeling to our American friends back home who've never left the country, let alone their home states. Some of the things we deal with as expats are things that can only be understood within the expat community. It's so important to surround yourself with people who feed off the energy you already bring.

And even with friends back home, there will be some who fan your flames in encouragement and those who blow it out from envy.

So surround yourself with like-minded people who you can not only learn from, but who can learn from you as well. You shouldn't be the smartest nor the dumbest person in your circle of friends. And when you find that you're the former, start seeking people who can challenge you.

This also isn't to say that anybody that disagrees with your lifestyle, ideology, or choices should be rid from your life. I think it's healthy to know people who are the complete opposite, because you'll force yourself to expand, develop, and defend your perspective when it gets challenged.

Opinions don't cost a thing as of yet. So we're all entitled to have our own, just like the ones I'm sharing in this book. You may disagree with every word I've said, in which case I applaud you for still reading, but at least you've been made aware of a perspective outside of your own.

Surround yourself with people who challenge you and encourage you, but most of all inspire you to tap into the potential of greatness you were destined for.

"Single & Ready To Wrinkle"

In some countries, being single at 26 is as taboo as being pregnant at 16. Yet falling into the former has somehow caused me more ridicule on the road.

"Where's your boyfriend?"

"Well, he kinda does this thing where he doesn't exist. It's adorable."

"Hello! What's your name?"

"I'm Gloria."

"Oh, I'm Single!"

Clever. *insert eye roll here*

Honestly, it's not that I can't have a boyfriend or a relationship. It's just the quality of the men I've met and the standards I'd like to have for a future companion put me back into this cozy ol' box of singledom.

But at least this box has wine. And cats. Seventy of them to be exact. And they're keeping me company.

Relationships are hard work! And heck, so am I!

When you've been single for this long, you almost forget how to function and coordinate with another person who feels like they need to have a say in every aspect of your life. Wait a minute— that's not a relationship at all. That's control.

I hate being controlled! Hence, why I'm slightly unemployable.

You see, the couple of times I was swept off my feet by a potential suitor, my brain did this thing where it completely shut down. Like, completely. I couldn't use it for days and it affected my work, my business, and ultimately my life.

Follow your heart, but take your brain with you. Why is it that most of us can only bring one? The two cannot coexist, I tell you!

It was then that I knew I wasn't emotionally available or ready for a relationship. I can't give my heart to two things when I want to be fully invested in one more than the other. I'm focused on my blog and growing my brand.

Life goals. What are yours? And why do they involve so many material things? I can't deal with these kinds of levels of incompatibility. Call me picky. Call me pathetic. Just call me in general! No, really. I'm hungry and I'd like to be taken to a fancy dinner somewhere.

You want to know how bad I am at flirting? Of course you do. Because a girl can't simply have it all and God's way of humbling me was by giving me manly feet, a slow metabolism, and flirtation skills similar to that of a toddler's—nonexistent outside of drooling, gibberish, and accidental farts. Oops.

One time in Barcelona, I met this Dutch guy at a bar, and he was of course Zeus-like and manly, as I reciprocated with my usual Goddess-like appearance and awkwardness. Nonetheless, he introduced himself and as I was so eager to speak and swooned by his presence that when he asked where I was from, I instead offered my name "Gloria!" and just a bit too excitedly at that.

Because only adults know that when you're asked a question, listening to it and forming a response would be the smart, adult thing to do. And because of awkward reasons, there was no way to recover from this blunder. So I had to make up a city called Gloria in California. Ya know, close to LA. I'm sure you've passed it on the freeway. So yes, I'm Gloria from Gloria, California, and I'm just going to walk away now.

In all honesty, bless the hearts of the men who try to keep up with the fast-paced, ever-changing souls of us female wanderlusters.

The quick wit, impulsive nature, and always evolving idea of what our lives should look like make them some of the most complex creatures to ruin, and yet grace, the dating scene.

We female solo travelers thrive in new environments, which may or may not include you, but if you are somehow in the picture, here are some tips to help ease the roller-coaster ride that dating a girl who loves to travel can be:

---

1 — She will value experiences over material things.

Skip the overpriced bouquet of flowers and take her to a hidden garden instead. You bring the wine and she'll bring the stories.

This will mean so much more to her than the decaying daffodils she would've snapped a picture of for Instagram before forgetting about it moments later. Because, Generation-[WH]Y.

---

2 — Don't pressure her with questions about the future.

The idea of "settling down" is slightly (read: very) terrifying. She knows she can't live out of a suitcase forever. But she's okay with pretending it's a possibility anyway.

She's okay without the infamous 5-year plan. It limits her possibilities because she knows opportunities arise just as quickly as they go.

---

3 — She wants you, but she doesn't need you.

Solo travelers, by nature, are independent and daring souls. They've navigated the most confusing of railways and survived horror stories from the most remote locations in the world.

She can hold her own with or without you, and despite the rumors of having sugar daddies funding her lifestyle, she only wishes she could be so lucky. Ha! But really.

---

4 — She has a home, but it's more of a feeling than a place.

Everyone has a home base they return to after a while of traveling. But because she's met so many kind and generous souls on the road, she can make a home wherever she goes.

The idea of having to fly thousands of miles to celebrate every major holiday is no longer a burden for her because she will make the most of any situation no matter where she is.

---

5 — Don't be overwhelmed by her circle of friends/acquaintances.

If she likes you, you won't have to worry about sharing her. But just know there are people all over the world who appreciate her presence just as much as you do.

So let her be free to reunite with the hundreds of friends she's made while traveling.

There's a certain type of energy she thrives from, and only fellow wanderlusters can truly feed that into her.

---

6 — Don't question her gut.

She questions it enough herself. She's a traveler. She's impulsive. She constantly yearns for more. Her savings account is depleting by the second (sorry, Mom).

Still, she continues on a path so few are able to go on because there's this fire that burns inside her and she wouldn't dare keep anyone around her who tries to put it out.

7 — *She doesn't succumb to societal pressures.*

Biological clocks and fads hardly exist to her. She tends to take what she has and make it trendy.

Often, she can be a trendsetter because of that, and if she's looking to make a decision, society is the last thing she'll turn to.

She was born to stand out and there are plenty of seats to be taken for those who are uncomfortable with that.

8 — *Be positive or be gone.*

Solo travelers have learned how to escape the three "D's" of travel: danger, death, and deportation. She stays optimistic because it could always be worse.

The last thing she needs is a cloud of negativity reminding her of every worst-case scenario and safety precaution.

She's a calculated risk-taker. She will always make sure the rewards outweigh the risks.

And as long as danger, death, or deportation have yet to halt her journey, don't add to the list and be a douchebag to ruin her winning streak.

9 — *Understand she's been single for a reason.*

She's learned through travel how short and fleeting life can be, and she wouldn't dare waste it on the wrong person, especially when that hinders the chances for the right one to come along.

It's easy to be in a relationship; it's hard to be in one of substance, maturity, and mutual growth.

She's okay ridin' solo for as long as destiny sees fit. Not to mention, she probably sucks at flirting. So there's also that.

She's a rare breed. She's constantly growing, changing, and evolving into the best version of herself, all while leaving her mark on the world.

She has a remarkable spirit that can lift even the darkest of souls, and you'll never have to question her loyalty because she makes it very clear where she stands on everything. She's not afraid to think for herself.

While she may seem like an intimidating package on the outside, first-class stamped and air-mailed to meet you in the most exotic of locations, just know that when and if you get this special delivery, she will truly be a gift.

"10 Things That Can Make A Catcalling Experience Less Creepy"

L et's not ignore the obvious here—as a solo, female traveler, unwanted attention will come.

And before anyone claims to enjoy the attention while it still lasts, honey, no. I won't give someone that power or satisfaction.

But what I can do is let you know how ridiculous you sound and flip the script by putting the discomfort back on you.

I'm not going to lie: It takes a bit of shamelessness to do some of these, but if you do it successfully, there's really no looking back. Also, you're welcome.

---

1 — *Stare In Disgust*

This is more so to throw them off and make them think they're even more repulsive than they know. They will be so concerned that you're disturbed by something on their face, so make sure you don't break character. And when you've bothered him enough, quickly laugh and walk away. He'll think twice about trying his antics again in the case that he happens to try it on another psycho like you.

Unless he's into that, no judgments here, you won't find a quicker way to turn him off and keep things moving if you pretend to be one thing on the outside and another thing on the inside. (Un)fortunately, all it takes for me to have a manly voice is some liquid courage or a lack of sleep. Both of which I usually get on a regular basis, so it really comes pretty natural. #blessed

3 — *Fart*

Again, this takes some skill here. You can fake it, or if you happen to summon the gods in that moment in time to deliver a bowel movement so strong that people will wonder if they just felt an earthquake, then you deliver that bad boy, fully bent over, cheeks spread (kidding), and release. I wish I could speak from experience about how awesome this would be, but I'll let you ladies take the lead on this and just tell me the results later. Even if it includes a lawsuit.

4 — *Burp*

This is also equally gross and severely frowned upon in many regions of the world. It can be quite the turnoff, especially in the Balkan countries (totally not speaking from experience here), and it's a great way to make sure a guy probably never gives you the time of the day, which, how convenient, because neither will you.

5 — *Fake-Call A Friend*

Without fully facing him, acknowledge how you just saw the grossest human being in the world. Describe him down to his bootleg sneakers about how bad he smells and how trees are working tirelessly to produce oxygen for him, and how he should apologize immediately. Say all of this loud enough for him to hear, without facing or speaking to him directly. He will feel SO foolish.

---

6 — *Politely Ask That You Need Help Looking For Decent Men In The World*

Acknowledge him enough to the point when he thinks he's got your attention, then throw him a curve ball and talk about everything you hate about men, describing everything he did, while politely asking him to point you in the direction of a real gentleman. Before he's even able to react, just suggest that it doesn't matter, because it's probably as far away from him as possible. *cue the catwalk exit*

---

7 — *Ignore Them, Blatantly*

This is pretty obvious and maybe the most common, but use this one especially when they've done so much to go out of their way and make their catcalling, hollering, and whistling heard. This will cause everyone but you to give this man attention, in turn making him look like a hopeless and desperate fool while you go about your day unbothered.

---

8 — *Suddenly Develop Tourette's*

This is also incredibly bold and I recommend having a couple choice beverages in your system beforehand, but nothing screams catcalling material like a sudden uncontrollable itch that's just a natural reaction when you're around such lame excuses for people. Twitch harder the closer he gets or the more he tries to talk and as soon as he stops, pretend you're miraculously cured and carry on about your day as normal.

---

9 — *Mock Their Words In A High-Pitched Voice*

I know you remember being twelve once. It was fun. It was annoying. And it was effective. Someone says something to you and you mimic their exact words in this ridiculously high-pitched tone that only intensifies just how foolish their words were to begin with.

---

10 — *Scream In Their Face*

Ahh, yes. Here come your psychotic antics again. I promise you'll thank me later. But nothing screams emotionally unstable (literally) quite like you, in his face, for no reason at all. He'll be dodging a bullet, hopefully not literally (looking at you, America), and you both will be better off because of it.

"How To Safely Hitchhike Abroad"

Now before you all remind me of the dangers of hitchhiking, I just want to let you guys in as to why I decided to try it.

The city I wanted to get to was a 30-minute drive and a $2 bus ticket away. It was not about the money. It was about challenging myself and gaining mental toughness and patience when put in a situation where I'm left vulnerable and with very little control.

I'm an Aries. We're bosses. Self-reliant. Independent. And we love to be in control! So I knew this wouldn't be easy despite my ability to adapt to new scenarios rather easily.

I'd also been asked many times for tips on this, and I always try to be the leader that can speak from experience, not inferences from other people.

A great life skill to have is awareness and detailed observational skills. Being able to pick up on vibes instantly is huge. And most importantly, allowing yourself to trust in the innate kindness of strangers.

The fear-mongering media have gotten away with propagating solely harm and danger about hitchhiking and so many other aspects of the world that keep people from traveling, and I hate it!

The honest-to-God truth is that you're more likely to win the lottery or get eaten by a shark than get physically attacked from hitchhiking.

And there are absolutely ways to hitchhike SAFELY. Having met 20+ hitchhikers in the last few months from Poland, Brazil, Belgium, and Canada, I want to thank them for inspiring me to push my limits and try this for myself!

I will never be a do-as-I-sayer, always a do-as-I-doer (RIP, English) because I want to teach you guys from a firsthand perspective. So here are some quick tips on how to prepare for your first experience.

1 — Look/Be Confident

Whether an hour has passed, whether you're hungry, or whether you had tacos for lunch and your bowels have internally started WWIII, you'd better stick that arm out as firmly as you can and act like your thumb is balancing your student loan debt.

Be shameless about it! People will judge and stare (and hopefully fall into a ditch and die, KIDDING!), but who cares?! Chalk this up as another adventure and testament to your bravery in life.

And even as the first car pulls over, you have the right to be as picky as you want. Yes, creeps and language barriers are inevitable, so make sure you learn a few phrases of the local language so that nothing will get lost in translation and it warrants no explanation.

2 — Location Is Key

After standing about 15 minutes in a busy location that was headed toward the main highway to Kotor, Montenegro, a local offered the advice of standing a bit further down the road so that I have a better chance of catching people who are almost certainly either driving to this city or passing it.

You also want to make sure you stand in front of a place that allows for them to pull over, because a two-lane double highway lowers your chance of a car stopping, because you've got crazy motorcycles and semis driving at high speed.

---

3 — *Have A Fun Sign*

Drivers have about 1.5 to 2 seconds MAXIMUM to read your sign. Make it worth their time! And even if they don't stop, they will laugh, wave, honk, and smile and I took all of these as "we would stop, but we're in a hurry, have no room, etc."

A couple hitchhiking friends have used signs like "I wear deodorant" to make the driver laugh and help negate the stereotype that hitchhikers are all dirty and homeless.

White cardboard also reads better than brown, so find a local bar, because they will definitely have most of their imported beer packaged with white cardboard insides. (What is life-changing knowledge for 500, Alex?)

---

4 — *Be Patient*

Remember, it's as much of a risk for them as it is for you. Give yourself three to five hours of daylight from the start of the time you begin standing. I gave myself a goal of getting picked up (lol, not like that) in an hour.

If all else fails, definitely have a backup plan. I knew I had a two-kilometer trek to a bus station or taxis passing by every five minutes if I felt myself getting tired.

---

5 — *Look Like You're Having Fun!*

Make them feel like they're the ones missing out on the party from not stopping.

If you look depressed and defeated, why would anyone want that pathetic and pitiful energy in their car? Energy is so contagious and it's important you're always adding to the positive energy of others and not taking away from it.

I recommend hitchhiking in pairs your first time around. I had a friend wait the first 30 minutes with me while I got a chance to piss my pants of nervousness, get over my initial panic, and just relax and have fun!

There are websites like HitchWiki.org that have compiled forums and sources of information from people who've hitchhiked in several regions around the world to help provide specific information, and whether you're trying it with a friend or by yourself, you're guaranteed to find yourself experiencing a whole new level of adventure!

"The Serena Williams Tour"

Incident #1

The first time I realized I was Serena Williams in another life came unexpectedly. I had no idea what an elongated joke this would turn into after the first time it happened.

I was traveling to Istanbul, Turkey from Bucharest, Romania via train and needed to pass through Bulgaria to make it happen. Lol, I love my life.

It was a pretty anticlimactic few days as we were in the middle of the refugee crisis and that region was affected pretty heavily by those seeking asylum.

Eastern European train travel in general doesn't have the greatest conditions. In fact, they were pretty horrific.

The conditions were so bad, our train broke down every few minutes. It took us four hours to go about 25 miles. But that didn't stop us from hanging our heads out the window while drinking Romanian beer, admiring Bulgaria's countryside views in our 100-seat cabin split amongst all eight of us, haha.

Then we finally reached the border and the border patrol took my passport for a few minutes. This didn't happen to anyone else, so I panicked a bit and came outside and heard them saying things in their native language and pointing at my passport. I nervously laugh along and ask, "Uhhm, what's so funny?" and they say, "Haha, ez bee-cos ju luke like Seh-veena Vee-liums." (Serena Williams) Ha, I wish.

Incident #2

Then there was Parga, Greece, Cinque Terre's slightly sexier cousin.

This town is a gorgeous and favored holiday spot by locals and other Balkan natives. You can come here with your family, have a romantic getaway with your +1, or just bask in your singleness like me, making romantic strolls to the ATM to invest in $1 gyros and 50-cent Greek beers.

And as a bonus, if you just slightly resemble a world-famous athlete like Serena Williams, you, too can enjoy the generosity of bottomless-pocketed locals who will thrust every cocktail down your throat (that's definitely what she said) and make sure you know that if you ever need a break in between Grand Slams and Wimbledon titles to "please come back and visit, because you are always welcome."

The owner not only asked for a picture, but I genuinely think he believed I was Serena, despite the fact that she was competing in the U.S. Open that very weekend.

He friended me on Facebook, which is where I first saw the picture we took in which he captioned, "I'm very excited to welcome Serena Williams in my bar today."

The picture amassed dozens of likes and comments from friends telling him to "buy her a drink for me" or "make her sign a tennis ball!" It was hilarious. And weird.

Seven cocktails later, I was ready to retire my crown and every tennis championship I'd ever won—or she'd ever one. Sorry, sometimes I get too into character.

Then along came the takeaway food owner across the street with a box of pizza for me. I never wanted the night to end.

Incident #3

So I had a friend from Las Vegas, Ireti, who said she wanted to visit me in Montenegro while she was vacationing up in Croatia. I told her to prepare for the red-carpet treatment as it's not every day Serena and Venus Williams visit Montenegro together.

She was a tall, skinny black woman who (in the eyes of foreigners) could definitely pass as Serena's older sister, Venus.

This town hardly sees one black woman on a regular basis, so I told her two just might cause the city to shut down.

Jokingly serious, it took but ten minutes before we were offered our first complimentary beer from a local bar.

Leaving the beach, we were then invited into another bar by the owners who asked for a photo before offering us shots of Rakija (basically regret in liquid form) and letting us know we were welcome any time.

Then came the funniest encounter when an elderly woman walking toward us in the opposite direction stopped dead in her tracks, grabbed her neck, let out an audible gasp, and sized us up and down. Looked very similar to a heart attack. We hope she's okay.

Throughout the day, we had men, women, grandparents, and kids jerking their necks to figure out who we were and why we were in Budva.

I vaguely heard "Seveena" (Serena) under someone's breath and knew that there was a good chance we definitely mirrored the Williams Sisters.

After a group of Russian teenagers mobbed us for photos, we couldn't help but laugh at the random, but all-too-perfect experience we had and will always remember Budva, Montenegro for.

For the remainder of my time in Montenegro, I figured I'd channel my inner-bootylicious tennis babe and continue milking her fame for every drink and meal it earned me—several.

Did I feel guilty in the end? Not really, because now if Serena Williams (the other one) were ever to make her way down to the Balkans, she'd already have an established group of businesses, restaurant chains, and bars who will have her (my) photo, her (my) signature, and a great reputation to uphold.

Thank you, Serena Williams. I owe you like 50 drinks and 20 meals.

"5 Habits I Had To Kick While Living In Europe"

Traveling helps you grow your tolerance and decrease your judgments. You learn to accept and appreciate all people, religions, and traditions as if they were your own.

From previously living in America all my life, it didn't take long for me to realize I had to kick these habits to the curb or suffer falling by the wayside. Adapting and making small changes on the road really do make a difference in the long run. Here were the habits I struggled with the most.

1 — *Spending Coins Like Quarters*

This one hurts a lot. Especially in the UK. We had a short four-year reign of the Susan B. Anthony dollar coin in America, which is hardly circulating anymore, and I think I've only ever seen two in my entire life.

Dollar coins just weren't a thing to me, and so spending GBP (£) in England like quarters in America hit me hard in the long run. I had to learn to stop devaluing coins like they didn't equal much, because my pounds were being spent left and right and I ended up accidentally doubling or tripling my spending habits because of this.

I never knew how popular the smoking culture was in so many areas of Europe. In some countries, I'd find myself being the only one who didn't partake in it in an entire restaurant or establishment.

I found myself inching out of circles and turning away from people who were talking to me, because I didn't understand how they saw nothing wrong with blowing their secondhand smoke in my face. I was disgusted.

But alas, it was their "culture." It's a social norm. They grew up around it and therefore have and will continue doing it for the rest of their lives. It's not so much a health risk to them as it is a social pastime.

I learned to cope with it and be social again, just making sure I wore my crappiest clothes and soaked them immediately after, to get out the smell out before I went to bed.

---

3 — *Feeling The Need To Settle Down*

It's not a secret that if you're in your 20s, half your friends are already married or engaged; the other half already have kids, and then there's you.

Everyone these days seem to find their significant others at younger and younger ages, and not that anything is wrong with that, but feeling pressured to catch up was something I had to kick.

I had to accept that we all live different lives and have different circumstances. My life is moving at a million miles an hour, and maintaining a relationship on the road might be the last thing I need right now.

It's all about timing and destiny, and I had to learn to fully accept that.

4 — *Not Making An Effort To Be More Globally Informed*

So many times I've met Europeans who knew more about American politics and history than I did. It was impressive and rather humbling. It's crazy how obsessed/concerned they can be with our national affairs.

It inspired me to keep better tabs on the global affairs in this world, because even though I might not be directly affected, it could help me understand and piece together the current state of international relations of countries as I travel.

5 — *Redefining Luxuries vs. Necessities*

Never did I think I'd ever find myself contemplating life through a series of things that I actually needed to survive versus what I merely enjoyed for leisure.

You see, hot showers, those are indeed a luxury. One I took for granted before I started traveling.

I almost cry happy tears at the sight of washing machines now, because I've gotten so used to hand-washing all my clothes.

And what I'd give to have any type of black hair-care products shipped to my doorstep on a monthly basis, my goodness!

And a decent Wi-Fi connection? Lord, some day. Because we all know Wi-Fi stands for Without Internet, Feeling Incompetent.

But alas, luxuries.

When you travel full-time, you're going through constant changes. But the more you can get at adapting to your surroundings and accepting things for what they are—especially when they're out of your control—the better.

PART FOUR

The Destination!

"Answers About My Nomadic Lifestyle"

From interviews with online publications to common questions I get from readers about my nomadic lifestyle, here's a quick compilation of some things that will help bring clarity and/or understanding about my life and all things travel-related about it.

From Nastasia Wong at DameTraveler.com

When did you fall in love with travel?

I was incredibly fortunate to have studied abroad my super-senior year in college, and that gave me my first taste of life across the pond. I never dreamed or imagined a life outside of the U.S. until I took my first transatlantic flight, which goes to show that you never know where life will take you, but the willingness to make bold moves is a good first step! It's amazing what one single experience can do to altering your perspective and forever changing the way you see life.

The people I meet and exchanging our stories. Every now and then, I have one of those surreal moments or encounters where I have to take a minute to catch my breath and fully process the beauty of the moment. Being in a foreign land, having this beautiful dialogue with a beautiful human about the most intimate aspects of life, and having just met 10 minutes ago.

Those moments inspire me to continue spreading my passion and love of life with others despite the ocean, language, or socioeconomic boundaries that try to keep us apart. Traveling is a constant dialogue between yourself and your soul, growing, learning, and challenging anything and everything you've ever thought about life. It's surreal.

How has a life of travel changed you?

It's turned me into a believer. A dreamer. A lover of all things, people, customs, traditions, cultures, languages, and lifestyles. It's opened my heart to crave a way of life I never knew I had an appetite for.

What inspires you most about this beautiful, complex world we live in?

How we are all far more alike than different. And no matter what language you speak or what part of the world you're from, there's a universal language of laughter, smiles, and love. There's also a genuine kindness in every person I've met and the willingness inside us all to help out a stranger is awe-inspiring. It makes the world so much more connected than we think.

And living in a digital age, it's easier than ever to hang onto these connections and the best part, to meet up again in another foreign land than where you originally met. We can all learn so much from each other, and the way I think today is a product of the beautiful conversations I've had with [then] strangers [now] friends, through traveling.

What's your best advice for aspiring wanderlusters out there?

Deep down inside us all, I think there's a budding wanderluster waiting to burst out of your body and explore this dynamic and amazing world around us. But that voice is constantly drowned out by the waves of our excuses that we tell ourselves, like not having the adequate funds or time.

Listen up, guys: The time will never be right, you will never have the "right" amount of money, and unless you possess magical powers to read the future, your tomorrows aren't guaranteed.

Traveling is living in its purest form and nothing in life is a better teacher than the lessons you learn and experience through traveling. I'm so inspired by my blog fans and readers because as long as there is a constant stream of questions in my inbox about ways to live abroad, I know I'm doing my job in helping inspire a future generation of global citizens and ambassadors of this world.

From Sienna Brown at LasMorenasDeEspana.com

Describe yourself in 3 words.

Passionate, creative, and awkward!

Who or what inspires your sense of personal style?

I would say fellow travelers and free-spirited people I meet. As a perpetual spender on all things travel, I don't have money to splurge on the latest trends, so I take what I have and make it trendy and I think it has a boho chic feel to it. Like if homelessness meets Urban Outfitters. Hahaha. I don't even know what that means.

What has surprised you most about European living?

How cheap and minimally people live. If the average person in America compared the cost of living, expenses, and everyday spending to that of a European country like Spain, they'd spend 50% less a month. You just don't need that much to live comfortably here, and I love that.

From Marta Rusinowska at A-GirlWhoTravels.com

What drives you to travel, besides the obvious such as experiencing new cultures? What do you hope (or have) experienced through travel?

I'd say the same things that drive me to live. My passion for life and people exceed far beyond my capacity to comprehend and I'm fueled by the fire that gets lit with every new soul, city, and culture I encounter. I want to breathe the air of unknown territories, dance with the dancers of remote locations, and dine with the locals of unfamiliar backgrounds. The compassion and understanding you develop on the road is something you can't be taught any way else.

Solo female travel is often portrayed as dangerous in the mainstream media. What is your number-one reason for women to travel solo?

It's so important to be an advocate for solo female travel as the world and mainstream media continue to push the image of danger and fear in the forefront. I think one of the most empowering responses I get in my inbox is from blog readers who tell me I've inspired them to take their first solo trip. That means the world to me, because to have that kind of influence on a complete stranger means I have the power and ability to see courage and bravery in people before they see it in themselves. I will always be a solo traveler before anything else, and a woman will never see her limits fully pushed and perspectives fully expanded until she sets off on an adventure on her own.

What's your biggest travel hack or secret?

BEING FLEXIBLE! It's not necessarily a hack, but hear me out. I only book my trips on one-way tickets, because I know how easy it is for plans to change or things to come up, so I try to go with the flow. A lot of times airlines or train tickets will go up and down depending on whether they need to fill seats, so I try to get a last-minute deal on my way back or reroute my journey toward another place that's super-cheap. It's a win-win, because I'm exploring for cheap and I'm able to keep traveling on.

This is starting to become a well-known trick, but search for flights in private or incognito tabs. Websites and search engines are collecting the cookies of your browsing history and raising flights to build urgency to get you to book the ticket! Don't get stuck paying more than you need to!

"Questions You Might Get As An African-American Abroad"

One thing about traveling as an African-American is that when you're mingling with the locals, there will never be a shortage of questions, concerns, and a variety of ways to politely insult your heritage. They'll range from weird and hilarious to tinkering along the lines of extremely offensive.

I asked a few of my African-American friends from well-traveled backgrounds to share some of their craziest questions or comments they've been told while traveling or living in another country. I also anonymously added in my own. Enjoy! Kinda...

"How does your hair stay braided like that? Can I touch it? Can my friend touch it?"

"If you're eating chocolate, how do you know when to stop?"

"Can I rub dirt on you? You won't be able to see where, right? Since you're the same color?"

"I bet you can sing really good. All black people can sing!"

"How come the top of your skin is black, but underneath (palm of hands) are white?"

"Do you wear sunscreen? Because, well...you don't really need—I mean, I don't know, do you?"

"Are you related to Obama?"

"OBAMAAAA! YES WE CAN!!!"

"Do black people own cars?"

"I want to go to Africa one day, after they finish dealing with their Ebola."

"How did you get your hair like that?"

"Did you know Michael Jackson?"

"Teacher, why are you so chocolate? I will eat you!"

"What are you?"

"I'm African-American."

"So what part of Africa is that?"

"Do you sunburn?"

"Can you dance like the people in the music videos?"

"Do you wash your hair?"

"Where in Africa are you originally from?"

"I'm from America."

"But where are you originally from?"

"My mom and dad are both Americans."

"Okay, but your grandparents?"

"They are also American. Just like Obama."

"Ahhh, you are Obama's daughter, Malia Obama?!"

"I wish."

"Do you know Serena Williams? She has hair like you, too!"

"Oh you're Michelle Obama? So beautiful!" (followed by her begging for money)

"Are you related to Michelle Obama?"

"I know you two! Venus and Serena Williams! Come, take a picture with me!"

"Why are your palms white? Are your feet white, too? You wash your hands too much. Black people have very white teeth. Why do you say you are black? You are not black. You are brown. You are from America? Impossible. How did you get there? You are from Africa. Black people are only from Africa."

"Do you wash your hair? Black people probably don't wash their hair. That's why it looks like that. You should wash your hair more and it will look like mine."

"Let's make babies. I want black babies."

A Chinese lady started following us. I kept telling my husband she was following us, so finally we turned around and she said "Beyoncé!?" and then held up her camera to take a picture.

"Do you prefer to be called blacks or African-Americans? Why do some of you say African-American but you have never been to Africa?"

"Do your people have cars in Africa?"

"Do you live with monkeys and other animals in Africa?"

"Don't touch or lean on my car, do you guys have cars and houses in Africa? Is that why you left Africa and came to Korea?"

"What part of Africa are you from?"

"I'm not from Africa, I'm American."

"We don't like Americans."

After failed attempts of getting me to go on a date with a man, I received an email that asked if I had a black woman to give to him, and that I would be paid very nicely.

"What are you? Because you aren't like black, black. You don't look like the Africans that live here."

"Black women have big butts because they like to have a lot of sex. The more sex you have, the bigger your butt gets." *brief pause* "Now stand up so I can see yours." (This is all in front of my son, so we got up and moved as far away as possible).

"You're from the USA? Ohhhh, your face is very dark!"

"Your skin is very different."

"I like black women."

"Will you be my Beyoncé?"

"I like basketball and hip-hop too, just like your people."

"You're African-American? You don't look black, look at your teeth, your nose, and your hair. It's not like mine." (from an African lady)

While in China, someone I met couldn't fathom black women existing. They knew black men do because of the NBA, but for some reason the idea of a black woman was just too confusing.

"Wow, your skin is so smooth and pretty."

"Teacher, are you Obama's sister?"

A student was turning my palm up and down. Then started chanting, "black, white, black, white."

"Your skin is softer than Koreans'."

On a train from Busan, two dudes came up to me and started a conversation with, "We like rap music."

On a bus in Korea, a lady started touching my hair saying, "Ohhh, ohhhh, sooo soft."

I was wearing my hair in braids and this Chinese man came up to me and said, "That's not your hair."

"Black people are so lucky and blessed. It's like they have music inside them, the way they can dance!"

At the gym in China a lady told me, "Your butt is not healthy. It's too large."

When my husband and I first started teaching at this school, some male students were walking behind us talking to each other. They said, "Wow. It moves! Yes, it's moving! Look!"

A woman walked up to me, grabbed my butt, and called it "delicious."

I was in Egypt admiring the pyramids for Winter Break and a group of 50 schoolgirls all turn around and start pointing, and then ran up to me to ask what part of Africa I was from. When my Egyptian friend responded with, "She's American," they lost it. For the next 10 minutes I was taking pictures with all these young girls who I guess have never met an African-American before.

I'm telling my kindergarten students what we will all wear for our performance the following day (white tops and black bottoms). I repeat this several times so they can remember. Then one student said, "But Ms. Ivy, your arms and face are black." *crickets from the whole class*

"It's okay, I can still wear a white shirt."

A Pakistani cabdriver asked me if I was from Africa. I told him, "No, I'm American."

"How can you be from America if you are black?"

"There are many blacks in America."

"But your parents or grandparents were born in Africa, right?"

"Yes, but hundreds of years ago."

(Then he looked at me as if he had won the argument.)

As African-Americans make up less than 5% of the entire U.S. study-abroad population, there's no wonder as to why some of these lingering thoughts are held by so many. As I've added my own personal experiences to the list, it's a subtle reminder that many older generations in foreign countries who were born before the time of leisure travel and mainstream media really have no reason to keep up with the Western world today. And most don't. So the things they learned in school back then still hold true for them today.

Not only can you be a pillar of knowledge as you represent the shade of skin that formerly carried weight on just one side of the spectrum, but you're able to share with others the uniqueness of your ethnicity.

Whether you're Latin-American, Indian-American, Asian-American, or any other first-generation American breed, you don't know what type of positive reinforcement you can be until you put yourself out there, travel, and change the way people view you and others like you.

Ignorance is only from a lack of firsthand experience, propagated stereotypes through the media, and miseducation from passed-down "knowledge."

So hi, world. Yes, I'm African-American. But that does not mean I was born in Africa. Yes, you can touch my hair if you ask—politely. No I've never met Obama...yet. Yes, you can randomly take a picture of me to send to your parents. Yes, you can also take a selfie with me for your friends. No, I'm not some type of foreign exhibit from a museum. No, I won't be your fantasy version of a "Beyoncé," but I can be your friend. Yes, I will gladly educate you about my country, and no I will not answer to chocolate, because I'm not food, I'm a person. Thank you.

"10 Things People Who Travel For A Living Want You To Know"

While we try to maintain a professional image for our online portfolios, we can't fit in every detail of our lives, especially the many struggles, sacrifices, and failures. So in an attempt to help bring transparency to the lives of those who travel for a living, here is a list of ten things we want you to know.

1 — Our lives aren't a nonstop vacation.

We actually never stop working. You guys have the luxury of clocking in and out of work. Most of us work seven days a week and find it hard to turn our work mode off, because every aspect of traveling can turn into work sometimes!

2 — This didn't happen overnight.

I know it'd make you feel better thinking it did, but the reality is that it took years and years of perfecting our crafts, investing in our skill sets, and growing our audience and fanbase. The beauty of the journey is knowing how much you had to fail before you won.

---

3 — *We don't know everything.*

Every now and then we'll get emails asking about what people should do in Aruba or Alaska, with the person just assuming since we travel a lot that we've been there, without even trying to search our blogs or websites first.

Yes, we travel often, but the world is massive and we've still got a ton of ground to cover, so don't assume we've seen it all! Also, it doesn't hurt to do basic research before asking us to plan your trips for you. Yes, we want to help, but we're not your travel agents.

---

4 — *Yes, there are jobs that exist that can work with your desire to travel.*

Yes, many of us still pick up odd jobs here and there to supplement our travels when we're running short. Traveling doesn't have to only be for vacations. You can travel somewhere and get a job in that country if you want to! The easiest way, of course, is through teaching English.

---

5 — *No, we're not rich; in fact, we're probably poorer than you.*

Especially if we're less than a year into our blogging, we're not rolling in any kind of dough. And most of the money we make gets funneled back into our blog and our brand somehow, and of course, our addiction to traveling.

6 — We are not Google.

We love to help others, but understand that Wi-Fi on the road doesn't always allow for immediate responses. So the messages you send us at 2AM telling us you're heading to London in 24 hours and "need" me to "respond ASAP" usually don't get the best responses, if any at all. Respect our time and our lack of Wi-Fi as well as the fact that your Google search engine is more accessible than we are.

7 — There's a good chance we've written a post that covers some of the exact questions you've asked.

I know you're eager to contact us, but browse our blogs a bit, research general topics, and meet us halfway; that way our conversations can be as efficient as possible! The answers, and then some, could've already been covered in a post we spent hours writing!

8 — There are daily sacrifices.

We sacrifice everyday comforts and live pretty minimally to continue to afford and fund this lifestyle. But we choose these sacrifices because our desire to travel means more. You can't have it all, but if you want to travel, understand that the sacrifices are necessary.

9 — We know you kind of hate us.

Yes, we know most of our friends tinker delicately on a short-lined spectrum between envious hate and genuine pride. People can be incredibly jealous, and it's honestly uncomfortable for us as we know that type of energy can quickly turn negative. Why is it so hard for people to be happy for someone who worked their way toward a lifestyle they wanted? We do everything in our power to show you how you can, too, so please don't spew off the jealous remarks.

---

10 — We're all just kind of guessing our way to the top.

Every now and then, no matter how successful we get, we question what the heck we're doing—as do our parents, close friends, and strangers. We'll go weeks feeling on Cloud 9, only to inevitably return to the internal dialogue of what the heck is next.

On behalf of digital nomads everywhere, we love what we do, and if you want it bad enough, you could be in our shoes, too.

"From College Grad To Traveling Nomad"

When I look at my degree and all the effort and time that went into producing it, I'm damn proud of that expensive piece of paper that defined so much of my being—before Sallie Mae reduced me to a puddle of tears, that is. But even still, my degree was a product and summation of years of dedication (procrastination) and studying. Some of my greatest friends and mentors came from Baker University and my study abroad experience; so again, nothing, and I mean NOTHING could ever replace my college degree.

So growing up, we're told that a college degree is what makes you stand out from the bunch. It's what'll give you the upper hand in the rabid pool of job-seekers in America. It'll put you in the elite group of distinguished college graduates who studied [and drank] their way to that hard-earned degree.

What they didn't tell me back in 2000 is that 15 years later, a college degree would basically be equivalent to a high-school diploma. With more universities and programs catered to helping first-generation college attendees succeed, college degrees come a dime a dozen, and it no longer puts me in front of the rat race.

And let's not get started on the jobs that require two or three years of working experience straight out of college, and never mind the fact that this is the exact experience you're trying to obtain, but you need to first find experience elsewhere before bringing that experience over here. Because, post-grad life. Because, America. Because, huh?

The number of people who can find a direct correlation between their degree and their jobs is slim. Unless you're going into specific fields of teaching, law, or medicine, then that business or communications degree will work at just about anywhere that's hiring, and you might get stuck working next to the guy without a G.E.D. yet making the same minimum wage.

Nonetheless, my degree did get me my first job abroad in the UK, but to be honest, it was my experience that landed me the position. It was the fact that I was there as a student, developed a relationship with the staff, and my skill sets in design, media, and photography were desirable assets for the Student Development Office.

Having a degree was a requirement for the job ad, but any degree would've sufficed because it was more my experience they were interested in. So case in point, because I had been abroad previously (oh hey, thanks passport) and had gone through the same course and experience that future students would be doing, it helped solidify me as a suitable candidate.

My college degree was Interdisciplinary Mass Media & Arts, because whatever it is I thought I wanted to do in life (which changed biannually), I thought this degree could be all-encompassing. I love to write, design, create, and do photography. But what kind of job or label do I fit under?

Therein lied my "problem." I've never felt I was defined by one title or label, which is why a degree was merely a ribbon on an already boxed package ready to be shipped. My degree makes me look better on paper. Maybe more sophisticated and educated in the eyes of employers, but the better part of me was formed and shaped from traveling the world.

Entrepreneurship is a curvy yet narrow field that some pursue and others look down on, because a lot of times we're told to "get a real job," which...I'm still not sure what that means.

Get a real job and complain about it every day when I have to wake up? Get a real job and waste my life away working 40+

hours for someone whom half the office doesn't even respect? Get a real job and convince myself that 50 years in the workforce will guarantee me all the savings I need for a comfortable retirement? But let's cross our fingers that my health, able body, and circumstances will allow me to do all my heart desires once those glory years come.

Again, when I was younger, I was given this clean-cut list of top-earning professions as if that were supposed to motivate me—to pick what made me money instead of what made me happy.

The thing is, when you're told to go into a career for the money, you lose sight of your purpose along the way. I truly believe the love of money is the root of all evil, and if you spend your life chasing it, you'll never have enough.

One of the scariest traits in a person is greed, because once they start loving their things and their money more than people, they've lost their human touch. Own your money, but don't let it own you.

If I haven't ruffled enough feathers by now, allow me to dive face-first into the bird's nest with this list of differences between a degree and a passport.

- A degree opens you up to a job.
- A passport opens you up to the world.
- A degree costs you years of debt/payments/savings.
- A passport costs you $110 (in America).
- A degree makes you think four or five years is enough to figure out your career.
- A passport makes you think four or five years is enough to figure out your life.
- A degree completes your résumé.
- A passport puts a stamp on it (please see what I did there).
- A degree puts you at the disposal of employers.

- A passport puts the world at your disposal.
- A degree teaches you how to finish your business in school.
- A passport teaches you that there's unfinished business in the world.
- A degree shows you've taken lots of exams.
- A passport shows you've taken lots of risks.
- A degree will fill you with pride.
- A passport will fill you with memories.
- A degree will help get your foot in the door.
- A passport will help keep you in the room.

If I had to choose one, I'd pick my passport over my college degree.

Having possession of both has allowed me to see the advantages of what one can get me over the other. My passport has afforded me a life I never thought my wallet could grasp.

My passport has changed the way I see the world. My passport has taught me to love harder, feel deeper, and think wiser. I have compassion and understanding for people, religions, customs, traditions, and lifestyles I never gave a second thought to prior.

A passport has opened me up to a world of discovery, adventure, and knowledge. My passport has single-handedly changed my life for the better, and if you told me to give up one or the other, I'd practically thrust my degree into your arms (along with a slew of debt) and bid thee farewell as I took off on another adventure.

Confession: I'm a college graduate, but I've used my passport more than my degree.

If my passport cost as much as a degree, it would still be the best investment I ever made. The most important things to know about life are learned outside of the classroom. Love, compassion, and open-mindedness are curriculums in the school of travel, and as far as I'm concerned, this kind of education is on a whole other degree.

"Becoming A Successful Travel Blogger"

What's so amazing about my travel blogging journey is that it all sort of happened by accident.

I started my travel blog in the winter of 2013 as a way for family and friends to follow my adventures.

I had no idea it'd turn into what it is now. I had no idea I'd get approached on the streets by people who recognized my face. I had no idea I'd be crossing corners of the world that felt so out of reach until I started taking steps to bridge the gap between my dreams and my reality.

I tell people all the time: If you want to be a travel blogger for the money, you're in the wrong business.

Being rich is GREAT! Obviously speaking from experience here...ha! Find something in life you genuinely love, stay passionate about it, and I promise the money will come.

Don't let money be a reward of hard work; let it be a byproduct. Happiness and fulfillment in life are the ULTIMATE prize.

The majority come into this business for the pure love of travel and inspiring others to see how beautiful this world is and how rewarding meeting people from other countries can be.

Did I start my blog with this specific goal in mind? Not really. But I knew that success is a product of two things: passion and downright hustle.

I had both. And I knew that it would only be a matter of time until this crazy idea manifested into something bigger.

People on the outside often fall in love with the idea of success but want to cheat their way through the process. It doesn't work like that, and it didn't work for me like that, either.

I could count on one hand how many people were reading my blog back in 2013, and I could even name them on my friends' list. It was pitiful.

I put up a new post once every other month or so and wasn't investing my time into building it at first. Just like anything else in life, you can't expect growth without proper nourishment, attention, and care.

The grind of being a full-time employee in England at the time set in hard. I was in an environment where I never really got off the clock. I lived where I worked and I worked where I lived, so personal time for blogging wasn't a priority.

And then when it came time to leave the country, I found myself in Barcelona on a one-way ticket five days later with a mere $100 to my name. Hashtag, ballin'!

A new environment was just what I needed to get my juice back and revamp my passion, but it all came crashing down when I received an email the next day saying my domain and hosting subscription were up for renewal. How much would that set me back?

$75.

$75 that I didn't quite have to spare.

"What a waste of time!" I thought to myself, ready to quit on it.

I invested in this big photo shoot with a good friend Joee Siebel from Moments of Grace Photography in Kansas, spent so much time creating and designing the perfect layout and invested so much energy into this little corner of the Internet that gave me a platform to share with the world.

What. A. Waste.

The smart and rational personal wouldn't have renewed that site.

But I did anyway. Yes, I'm neither smart nor rational giving my circumstances.

I thought long and hard and figured that if it was important enough to start, it was important enough to finish.

I wouldn't call myself a "Professional Risk-Taker" if my life didn't involve taking risks...time and time again.

By this point, being broke was nothing new for me. I'd have phases of success, lapses in responsible spending (thanks travel addiction), and I'd always somehow find myself back at Square 1.

But I never stayed there for long. And I knew there was still potential for this blog to reach a larger audience and continue opening doors for me.

So I renewed my subscription and started staying up late to begin writing again.

But not just about anything—about things that people could really relate to. Funny things, strange things, deep things.

I wanted to blog beyond the surface of the content other travel bloggers were putting out. I wanted and needed to stand out to get my voice heard.

And that's when publications such as Matador Network, Huffington Post, and Elite Daily all started publishing my work a few months later.

It was almost history from there.

With their combined audiences of several million across the globe, my name spread like wildfire and my blog views jumped from 12,000 to 120,000 in a matter of days. So many new people a month on my site, reading my articles, learning my story. WHOA. It felt surreal and I couldn't quite grasp that number.

It was June 2015 when my biggest article in Huffington Post went viral, and it took me two weeks after that to pack my bags and decide to become fully nomadic because of all the doors, sponsorships, and companies who wanted to work with me since then.

Where would I be today had I given up on my precious blog? I'll thankfully never have to find out!

Guys, don't give up on your dreams just because they didn't happen overnight or "overyear." If it's worth it, it won't come easy, and if it's easy, it's not really worth it.

It gives me chills to think about what would've happened to my career had I not renewed my blog, but luckily I'll never have to find out!

"Don't Judge A City By Its Cover"

I always get a bit disappointed when I hear a tourist complain about a city like Athens.

"It's too dirty!"

"So much graffiti!"

"Greek people are rude!"

But I've been to Athens ten times now, so my experience is a bit deeper than the average 24-hour jaunt to the Acropolis and back.

As tourists and visitors to a country we don't inhabit, it's SO IMPORTANT to put things into perspective and remember that these cities and countries owe us NOTHING.

They do not exist for our hedonistic, Instagrammable pleasures.

These are places people live in. And here we come disrupting their daily commutes, trashing their streets, and keeping them up at night with our antics.

And you expect them to bow at your feet so they can wake up to your puke on their front door the next morning?

At minimum, when you're visiting foreign countries, you should be making deliberate efforts to know the basics of their language.

HELLO

GOOD MORNING

PLEASE

EXCUSE ME

THANK YOU

They go a long way, I promise.

For Greek people who don't work in the tourism industry and aren't benefiting from us being there, they don't owe us smiles or red-carpet treatment.

But every time I come to Athens, I've come to expect it, because I've learned the way to their hearts.

No matter what part of the city I'm in, I can always expect to see an elderly man sitting on a corner, just kind of letting time pass by.

As I catch his eyes trying to figure out where I from, I shout a hearty, "KALIMERA!" (Good Morning) his way and immediately a grin of the gods appears and he responds double time in shock and happiness, "KALIMERA, KALIMERA!" and we exchange a very brief but beautiful moment of our days.

Athens is a city with character. A city with pain. But ultimately, a city with a story. But it's up to you whether you get to read its colorful chapters or just be content judging it by its cover.

"10 Things I Wish I Knew Before I Started Traveling"

I've now spent over 1,000 days traveling and living abroad, and while some of those days I feel equipped to run a nation and other times I'm a mere breakdown away from resorting to Pampers, the happy medium in there reminds me that the growth has been incredible over time.

And for those who are about to embark on long-term travel for the first time, I hope this can help give you some insight as to what there is to know about the crazy world of travel.

---

1 — *A%$holes have no ethnicity, religion, or location. They're everywhere.*

Just the other day I was flipped off by a teenager on a bus. No reason. Maybe he thought it'd combat his bad day (read: micropenis syndrome) or something.

Then there was that other time a robust French lady shoved me out of the way for not opening the Metro doors fast enough in Paris.

And oooh my favorite, the American guy I met in Germany who told me to avoid Turkey like the plague, because he's "pretty sure that's where all the terrorists are."

le sigh

So whether I'm being cursed at for not walking fast enough in London or being looked at like dirt in Prague, a%$holes are (un) fortunately populated in every nation in the world.

God didn't discriminate. He made sure every country would have to tolerate these buffoons, and whether their a%$holery was gradually developed or a trait they were born with, let's just stop trying to make it our problem and let Darwinism take the lead with their existence.

So when you encounter one on the road, don't take it personally or allow them to ruin an entire destination or travel experience for you.

---

2 — Become a "YES" gal. They make for the best stories.

I met a guy named Dace from San Francisco while traveling in Jordan, and when we were swapping stories, he reminded me of the importance of being a "yes" man.

And how saying "yes" to every offer and conversation led to one of the most unforgettable days he's ever had while traveling. And I couldn't agree more.

Invited for lunch by customs officers at the border in Cyprus? I said YES.

Climb a dangerously steep, massive rock to watch the sunset in Petra? I said YES.

Explore a new city with someone you know from Instagram? ALWAYS SAY YES.

---

3 — Learn to let the universe play its course.

Missed your flight? It happens! Stay an extra day and do something ridiculous and unforgettable.

Get super lost? Good news! There's something everywhere you turn, so you're never technically "lost," just completely opposite of where you initially intended to go. ;)

The hot guy you met has just left? No worries! He probably has herpes or a girlfriend and was looking for an excuse to cheat on her. Dodged a bullet there, soldier. Chat it up with the other guy who's been eyeing you instead.

Whether it's patience, resourcefulness, or destiny that the universe is trying to show and teach you, allow it to do its job.

If everything always went as planned, we'd all be billionaires, right? :P

---

4 — *Surround yourself with like-minded travelers.*

As someone who spends her days constantly pouring inspiration, motivation, and empowering words into the lives of others, you get to a point where you exhaust all your energy and need to be refueled by the words and inspiration of like-minded people.

If you drain your mind of all the hope and encouragement you constantly give others, there's nothing left for you.

Seek mentorship and surround yourself with those who fan your flames, not extinguish them.

---

5 — *Don't ignore your anxiety/stress/depression.*

Life happens to everyone, and it's important to look after your mental health just as much as your physical health.

Don't ignore your depression if/when it comes.

Sometimes, there will be no cause of it. Sometimes, you won't know whom to talk to. Sometimes, you won't want anyone to talk to. But be sure to do something that's actively combating or fighting it.

You are not above getting help for anything you go through just because your life is coveted or romanticized by others.

---

6 — *Know your privilege and don't abuse it.*

Whether it's your privilege of traveling without visas based on your nationality, your privilege of not getting randomly stopped and checked for papers, or even your privilege that allows you to afford this lifestyle.

Keep your privilege in check and don't ever mistake it as an unwavering right.

---

7 — *Call your mom.*

Check in with her as often as possible. Any way you can. Calls. Texts. Photos. Skype. Whatever.

There is no such thing as over-calling the woman who brought you into the world that you're currently exploring.

---

8 — *Document everything. In multiple ways.*

Journal. Blog. Video. Photos. Letters. Postcards. Stamps. Anything!

It'll be SO valuable (for you) down the line.

The one thing you're promised is your nows and todays. So document them!

Remember them in their purest form by writing and recording those moments you want to keep forever.

I wish I took more video of my travels back in 2012. Video is as raw as it gets and whether you do anything with it or not, you'll have something to laugh and reminisce over years from now when Facebook reminds you that this cyber gold still exists.

---

9 — Don't confuse a magical moment for a magical guy.

Ah, yes. The inevitable. Falling in love on the road.

You're sitting on a hilltop, overlooking the sea, fireworks lighting up the sky from some random local festival that gave you another excuse to drink, and you're sharing that moment with a guy you met a few hours ago.

All of a sudden, you're planning out your exotic happily-ever-after when he'll just turn out to be a miserably-never-again.

You ignored the red flags, because when in Rome, right?! Wrong. Because you're in Barcelona. But also, no. Lol.

Follow your heart, but take your brain and morals with you. I promise you, the two can coexist despite what our *Jersey Shore* generation wants you to believe.

---

10 — Travel for more than just the fun of it.

Travel to learn. To challenge yourself. To earn trust. To make friends. To lose friends. To experience heartache. Poverty. Refugees. Corruption. Politics.

Travel to change more than just your profile picture, because there is so much to gain from this invaluable experience.

"A Journey To Your Heart"

Traveling solo has allowed me to do a lot of self-reflection—maybe too much! But over the last few years, I've learned so much from people and places that I decided to share my top 25 pieces of advice for anyone and everyone wanting to chase their dreams, live a happier life, or just make the most of every moment they're given.

1. Do something that pays the bills and something that makes you happy. Then repeat this cycle until the latter does both.

2. Keep a journal or diary documenting the happiest moments of your life and save it to be read at the end of the year, when you're stressed, or you just need a reminder of your purpose.

3. Whatever happens in certain phases of life, it'll either be a good time or a good story. Embrace them both.

4. Find a free activity that you enjoy and do it weekly.

5. Have a go-to song that puts you in the greatest mood and download it to your phone to be played at least once a day.

6. You know that thing that scares you? Do it anyway.

18. Regularly sleep at least seven hours a night (unless you're in college, then LOL, never mind).

19. If you wouldn't scream it in a public room full of strangers, it probably doesn't make a good Facebook status.

20. Never apologize for your confidence, especially if it's something that's been recently acquired. In a generation where depression, suicide, and self-esteem issues are running rampant, how dare someone try to knock you for being 100% happy in your skin? Own that ISH, my friend.

21. Give to the homeless more times than not. If not money, then a smile or simply compassion. Not all of them got there on their own.

22. Have an outfit at your disposal that would make a snowball melt in Alaska.

23. Don't let the size of your dreams intimidate you.

24. Come to terms with the fact that any issues other people have with you are none of your business. You could be the kindest, most giving, and loving person in the world and someone will find a way to have a problem with that. The self-hate and bitterness others have for themselves needs to be projected on others to keep them satisfied. This disease is only contagious to other self-hating victims. Criticism knows no limits in a world where everyone's a critic! You could be the ripest peach in the bunch, but there will always be someone who hates peaches. And that's not your problem!

25. And most importantly, "Don't feel entitled to anything you didn't sweat or struggle for," my favorite quote by Marian Wright. Life happens to everyone, but the world owes you nothing. Fight for what you want and pay for it with your own sweat and tears. It becomes so much more rewarding that way, too!

7. Despite what your family or close friends might think, you're exactly where you're supposed to be.

8. Go on a solo trip somewhere. Take your camera, a notebook, and a one-liner that will serve as a conversation-starter with strangers.

9. Cook more at home and eat out less. The bonding you have with yourself, family member, or significant other is much more intimate than that in a public setting. You'll also save a good chunk of money to be better spent on life experiences or, ya know, travel.

10. Never forget how to be a kid and never let the magic, mystique, and mystery of the world stop amazing you.

11. Instead of online dating, try online friending. Friend someone you've met online for the simple purpose of having someone you can go with on walks, community events, workouts, or other various hobbies. There's so much pressure put on romantic relationships; let's pursue friendships and playmates instead.

12. Stop hating on your friends' successes/relationships/jobs/marriages. The bitterness can be felt and smelt a mile away. And dat sh*t stank.

13. Stay humble and never forget where you came from, and especially those who were there for your struggle.

14. Be your own source of comfort, inspiration, and motivation.

15. Never stop dreaming.

16. Do what you love despite what your wallet might suggest. Money is an illusion. It comes and goes. There will always be ways to make it and spend it, so don't waste your life being a slave to the almighty dollar.

17. Find out what your worst quality or characteristic is, and work at it daily. Strive to be best version of yourself as possible.

"The Road Less Traveled"

The road less traveled...

Is lonely.
Dark.
Confusing.
Narrow.
Long.
Rocky.
Mysterious.
Full of detours.
Deceptive.
Rewarding.
Incredible.
Inspiring.
Magical.
Empty.

The road less traveled will never be crowded. Go the extra mile with work and you'll go the extra mile in life.

"From Excuses To Excursions"

Life gives you two things to be happy about—the day you were born and the day you figured out why.

If you're still searching for your "why," then I encourage you to spend some time alone and do some soul-searching.

Everyone has a special gift they can contribute to making this world a better place, and your gift may or may not be a solo trip away from discovery.

Life isn't about chasing perfections. In fact, I'd rather make mistakes than fake perfections. People can mock your failures all they want, but nobody can take away from your effort and willingness to try to succeed.

What floats your boat doesn't have to sail someone else's ship. Learn to live with the idea that your life shouldn't warrant other people's approval. There are people out there that want to see you drown, so don't confuse an extra paddle for an anchor.

Whatever greatness you were called for and whatever means you choose to go about finding it, I encourage you to never stop believing in yourself and the greatness you're capable of.

If I could turn my excuses into excursions, then the next step is helping you guys do that, too.

Epilogue

Congratulations! You've made it to the end of the most personal thing I own—my innermost thoughts. You've just traveled on a journey with me that no plane ticket could buy.

The destination is full of rewards, it's full of discovery, and most importantly, it's full of happiness—the one thing people spend all their life trying to buy through temporary fads and material items but never truly find.

The scary yet inspiring thing about life is that no one knows how long their time on Earth is. But when that day comes for me, I'll have this book to serve as my legacy. My legacy that I set out to do something great in this world—to inspire people's minds and move mountains with my words that will live on far after I do.

Whoever you are and wherever you are, know that you're destined for great things. How do I know this? Well, you finished this book! It's not for small-minded people, and if it sparked a fire of desire to be greater, then act on it now! Time waits on no one!

If I can ask one favor, though, please email me at _Globetrottin-Glo@gmail.com_ with your honest feedback, critique, and thoughts about this book so I can keep for future reference!

I also believe in the power of word-of-mouth marketing and how it serves as the truest and purest form of advertisement out there. We trust our circle of friends before people who pay millions to slap ads in our faces.

So if you loved this, I mean truly loved it, please feel free to pass on the link of the e-book with your friends on Facebook by sharing: *http://TheBlogAbroad.com/ebook* and please tag me as well! It'd mean so much to me and I can't thank you all enough for taking the time to allow me to share a very vulnerable and precious part of my heart with you all.

I love you all.
Thank you and God bless.

With Love,
Glo

ABOUT THE AUTHOR

Gloria Atanmo is the best friend and enabler everyone needs in their life. She's a force of nature and risk-taker who's on a mission to show others that there's a world of knowledge out there that simply can't be taught in a classroom.

She's fought to overcome the many obstacles life has thrown her way, mastering the art of calculated risk-taking, putting herself out there to fail over and over again until the universe finally caved in.

By textbook definition, she was going to succeed by way of insanity.

Through her relentless pursuit and hustle of discovery and exploration, she went from making excuses to taking excursions, turning internal fights into external flights, itching to shape the better part of her existence through travel. And encouraging others to do the same.

She believes if she's not living life on the edge then she's taking up too much space. She wants her fellow daredevils and rebels to read this book and feel empowered to explore a life far outside of their comfort zones to live the life of their dreams as well.

Whether you're into travel or not, she wants you to finally take on your thing. That ONE thing that sets your soul on fire. The thing you can't stop dreaming or thinking about. Because she did three years ago. And she's been fanning those flames ever since.

ABOUT THE PUBLISHER

Thought Catalog Books is a publishing house owned by The Thought & Expression Company, an independent media group based in Brooklyn, NY. Founded in 2010, we are committed to facilitating thought and expression. We exist to help people become better communicators and listeners in order to engender a more exciting, attentive, and imaginative world.

Visit us on the web at
www.thought.is or www.thoughtcatalog.com.

Follow Thought Catalog on Instagram
instagram.com/thoughtcatalog

Read More Amazing Books
thoughtcatalog.com/books

THOUGHT
CATALOG
Books